"Brutal honesty! Authentic vulnerability! Finally, a painfully funny book about a subject many have written about but few really understand. This book is the kind of stuff we rarely see in the land of politically correct Christianese. Please, people, listen to Kerri and Matthew! Learn from their plethora of mistakes!"

— DREW MARSHALL, host of *The Drew Marshall Show*, Toronto, Canada, www.drewmarshall.ca

HOW TO RUIN YOUR DATING LIFE

A CHRISTIAN'S GUIDE FOR AVOIDING [ALMOST] EVERY MISTAKE IN THE BOOK

MATTHEW PAUL TURNER & KERRI POMAROLLI

OUR GUARANTEE TO YOU

We believe so strongly in the message of our books that we are making this quality guarantee to you. If for any reason you are disappointed with the content of this book, return the title page to us with your name and address and we will refund to you the list price of the book. To help us serve you better, please briefly describe why you were disappointed. Mail your refund request to: NavPress, P.O. Box 35002, Colorado Springs, CO 80935.

The Navigators is an international Christian organization. Our mission is to advance the gospel of Jesus and His kingdom into the nations through spiritual generations of laborers living and discipling among the lost. We see a vital movement of the gospel, fueled by prevailing prayer, flowing freely through relational networks and out into the nations where workers for the kingdom are next door to everywhere.

NavPress is the publishing ministry of The Navigators. The mission of NavPress is to reach, disciple, and equip people to know Christ and make Him known by publishing life-related materials that are biblically rooted and culturally relevant. Our vision is to stimulate spiritual transformation through every product we publish.

ISBN-13: 978-1-60006-139-4
ISBN-10: 1-60006-139-7

Cover design by The DesignWorks Group, Tim Green, www.thedesignworksgroup.com
Cover image by Getty
Creative Team: Nicci Hubert, Kathy Mosier, Arvid Wallen, Pat Reinheimer

Some of the anecdotal illustrations in this book are true to life and are included with the permission of the persons involved. All other illustrations are composites of real situations, and any resemblance to people living or dead is coincidental.

Unless otherwise identified, all Scripture quotations in this publication are taken from the *Holy Bible,* New Living Translation (NLT), copyright © 1996, 2004. Used by permission of Tyndale House Publishers, Inc., Wheaton, Illinois 60189. All rights reserved. Additional version used is the HOLY BIBLE: NEW INTERNATIONAL VERSION® (NIV®), Copyright © 1973, 1978, 1984 by International Bible Society, used by permission of Zondervan Publishing House, all rights reserved.

Turner, Matthew Paul, 1973-
  How to ruin your dating life : a Christian's guide for avoiding (almost) every mistake in the book / Matthew Paul Turner and Kerri Pomarolli.
    p. cm.
  Includes bibliographical references.
  ISBN-13: 978-1-60006-139-4
  ISBN-10: 1-60006-139-7
  1. Single people--Conduct of life. 2. Dating (Social customs)--Religious aspects--Christianity. I. Pomarolli, Kerri L., 1973- II. Title.
  BV4596.S5T87 2007
  646.7'708827--dc22
                          2007017331

Printed in the United States of America

1 2 3 4 5 6 7 8 / 11 10 09 08 07

FOR A FREE CATALOG OF NAVPRESS BOOKS & BIBLE STUDIES,
CALL 1-800-366-7788 (USA) OR 1-800-839-4769 (CANADA).

CONTENTS

ACKNOWLEDGMENTS

FROM MATTHEW:

I would like to thank:

- Jessica for being my passionate wife. [I love you more than the sun.]
- Kerri for jumping into this project with nothing short of your all.
- Nicci for your friendship and for your editing guidance.
- Kathy for your meticulous copyediting and for your kind and thoughtful spirit.
- NavPress for inviting me to be a part of its family of writers; it's an honor.

And big appreciation to all who read these words.

FROM KERRI:

First of all I'd like to thank the Academy for all their votes. Oh, wait, that was the wrong speech.

For this book project I'd like to thank Kris, Kathy, and the rest of the NavPress crew who made this project a reality and were great in the process. Thank you to Nicci for her editing and Matthew for asking me to be a part of this.

Thanks also to my parents, family, and brother, Mark, who had to live through all of these dating disasters; my ex-boyfriends, without whom there would be no book; my girl-friends who got me through every one of these relationships in tact; my "Mighty Women" and all my prayer warriors, who've been truly amazing; and my mentors, Maritza and Cathy, who received many late-night phone calls and never complained.

Thank you to the incredible Rhonda Boudreaux, the best publicist/mom in the entire universe. She does not know the meaning of the word *rest* [which is why we're friends]. Rhonda, none of these projects would be completed without your prayers, your shoulder to lean on, and your infinite wisdom and dedication.

Of course I thank my Father in heaven because he's given me so much comedic material in my dating life to work with. But he's good because he answers prayers and gave me this crazy Korean comic named Ron McGehee to live happily ever after with. I love you, Ron, and I'm sorry you have to read another dating book about my ex-boyfriends. I promise this is the last one, honey!

LET'S DTR,* SHALL WE?

AN INTRODUCTION

Hello, single people who also happen to be Christian! Oh, we know you absolutely hate being referred to as Christian *and* single in the same sentence. Who knows why, but some church people make the combo of being Christian and single seem more like cancer or debt than a simple reality that normal people experience — hence the gag reflex that tends to follow the term *Christian single*. That reflex is especially strong for those of you in your mid to late twenties and still, as of this moment, not attached. [*You're the real freaks.*] On the other hand, there are the rare few who always think of being single as something positive. [*Can you imagine?*] Reasons for their contentment vary, of course, depending on their personalities.

---

* For those of you unfamiliar with this term, *DTR* means "define the relationship."

But they might very well include these:

- They're young and enjoy the dating scene. [That will probably change sooner or later.]
- They have this condition — most call it the fear of making a commitment — and it keeps them *always* on the prowl. [Yeah, people they've dated hate them.]
- Being single helps ensure that they're available whenever their church goes on missions trips or participates in other ministry opportunities.

Okay, so you probably get the point. Being a single Christian has its stereotypes, including the "bitter Christian single" and the "Christian playa." Another of these stereotypes is the prevalent but less talked about "Christian-dating-book reader." These folks read all those books that are meant to help the "dating impaired" find the right "moves" to ensure that "true love" will [or at least will have a chance to] eventually "happen." But as our friends in this category know, Christian dating books can sometimes make the process of dating even more complicated.

So then why are you holding another book about dating? You can't help yourself, can you?

Kerri and I agree that being a Christian single among other single Christians out there can be dangerous for one's health. We know because, like you, we have made every mistake in the book.

Personally, of all the people I have dated, I feel most awful about my relationship with a girl named Laura. As was the case with most of the women I dated when I was between the ages of nineteen and twenty-eight, I had every intention of marrying Laura. And in addition to being sure that I would marry her, I was privileged to know this information from the moment I laid eyes on her.

One day, just after I had finished nominating myself in front of the entire college for some random student board, Laura walked up to me and smiled. Little did I know that behind that beautiful smile of hers was a psychotic young woman who had been tormented by mean-spirited men. And behind the strong will and confidence she admired in me was a spoiled brat who fell in love with needy women way too quickly.

Oh, we were such a sad pair. We met on a Tuesday, and by that following Saturday we were rolling around on her bed [fully clothed, of course]. I mean, heck, we were Christians attending a Christian school; we weren't going to go *that* far. Laura and I ended up dating for a total of eighteen months over a period of two and a half years, which included three breakups, two get-back-togethers, and one random make-out session that happened after our last breakup.

Why do Christians do that to each other? Why do we have such issues finding love? I mean, even those of you who have experienced healthy relationships in the past were obviously just clumsy enough to mess it up, or else you wouldn't be reading this book. What's ironic is that we're followers of Jesus; aren't we supposed to be enlightened when it comes to building relationships?

If you're anything like Kerri and me, you probably don't need this book; you probably know exactly how to ruin your dating life. If you're a girl, you've probably experienced the inconsistencies and egos of the Christian male. And if you're a guy, you've probably encountered a few too many Christian girls who can't decide whether they want to be the virgin Mary or a Pussycat Doll. The oddities that happen when Christians roam the dating scene are as numerous as the books on Christian dating, and more than likely the last thing you feel like doing is reading *another* book about Christian dating.

Nevertheless, you're here, reading this book. But the good news is that this book isn't the same old Christian dating book. So hold on to your *Purpose Driven Life*s and your *effortlessly* tattered Bibles; you're in for quite the reading experience as Ms. Pomarolli and I bring you up to speed on the most perilous pitfalls of Christian dating. You've probably engaged in more than one. But it's okay; that's why you're here.

You know the story of dating books: They're almost as annoying and needy as our exes. And like the topic they cover, they are just as complicated at times. I mean, think about it. Whether you're learning that *he's just not that into you* or you're journeying toward *understanding women* or you're wanting desperately to believe that *dating rocks* or you're experiencing any of the various other issues that happen in dating, the books available in the mainstream market have all sorts of ideas to help you not only pinpoint your most obnoxious dating problems but also navigate through the ups and downs of the dating scene. And, of course, those ups and downs might be as gentle as a Sunday drive or as frightening [or thrilling] as a roller-coaster ride at Great America. Sometimes both.

I'm not exactly sure why, but dating is just one of those topics that gets complicated. I suppose it makes sense, really.

When you're looking for a relationship that will last a lifetime, the process can certainly give the ole emotions, pride, heart, and, not to mention, wallet a roller-coaster ride of experiences.

Let's face it: Though the word *complicated* certainly fits when trying to describe dating, it doesn't begin to define the personal stories we encounter while venturing out on the dating journey. The situations and circumstances we come across while dating can't be explained away with one easy definition or overused word. I believe that's why when it comes to talking about dating, lots of emotions and opinions arise. These emotions and opinions often make us question whether or not we can actually survive another date, another day of waiting for that phone call, or another DTR.

Believe me, Kerri and I know a good bit of what you're walking through; between the two of us, we've more than likely lived through every one of those little dating quandaries you're thinking about right now. We've experienced the gamut of the frustrations, breakups, mistakes, going-too-far problems, and, thankfully, some of the joys of dating too. And maybe that's why we think we're able to help a little.

I think we both learned the hard way that when it came to dating, the problems were personal. Yes, it was usually *us* with the problems, which was a very good thing since we couldn't actually have had any success in changing anyone but ourselves. That's not to say we didn't waste a good deal of time trying to change everything and everybody else, but more often than not we failed — and failed miserably. Why? Because most of the issues we encountered in dating were "me" problems, not "everybody else" problems.

[But we'll get to that soon enough.]

Here's the deal: Kerri and I are about to tell you exactly how to ruin your dating life.

Not heal it. Not make it into a path toward ecstasy. Not save it. Not give you an excuse to keep living it.

We want to show you how to ruin it. If we're in the ballpark, you've probably thought by now in your little reading adventure, *Um, how will ruining my dating life be helpful?* That's a good question. But allow me to be frank. Kerri and I have never dated you, so it would be impossible for us to comment on what kind of a date you are. However, we can only assume that since you are reading this book, there's a pretty good chance you have at least a couple of issues to work through before you can truly consider yourself date-worthy. I know that might seem like a harsh statement, but face it: You're not perfect.

Anyway, it's valid to inquire why learning how to ruin your dating life is a good thing. The short answer is this: Christians ruin their dating lives and don't even know it. So if we bring your bad habits to light, the hope is that you'll see your deeds and turn from your sins. You'll find a place of humility and feel a new sense of promise for your future. Because as things are, Christians just aren't that great at dating. I completely realize, however, that all the dating problems in existence aren't exclusively *Christian*. Muslims, Scientologists, and even atheists are prone to being a bit inept when it comes to pursuing a significant other. Thank God, right? However, unlike Muslims, Scientologists, and, yes, atheists, Christians are the only ones who have hundreds upon hundreds of books, seminars, websites, radio shows, advice columns, and experts to help us become successful in this pursuit. I'm not exactly sure what that means, but it hints at the possibility that, for some reason, we make more mistakes than others.

But according to popular opinion, dating is supposed to be fun! So why is it that many of us do whatever is necessary to make it not fun? I think it's because we worry: *What if I end up still single by the time I'm thirty-five?* We process: *If a guy hasn't responded to my e-mail within twenty-four hours, does that mean he doesn't like me?* or *If a girl says she's busy on Friday night, should I just assume she's not interested?* We pray: *God, please send me a hot boyfriend [or girlfriend] so I can stop being miserable and terrified of a future alone, spent in singles' groups.* And then there are times when we do all three — worry, process, and pray — at the same time. We can be such whiners.

I know Christians *are* getting together and living happily ever after — it's happening all the time. [This is probably a good time to mention that Kerri and I have both recently gotten married . . . but believe us, it took *a lot of time and energy* to get there.] We know — *from experience* — that dating is not easy. And more than likely you've experienced the not-easy part too. So Kerri and I present to you a book that tries to make your long story a lot shorter.

Enjoy.

ISSUES:
NOT HER, NOT HIM, BUT YOU

Let's begin this first section with a question. It's an easy one.

Why do you date?

I (Matthew) know that seems pretty basic, but it's something I believe is worthy of your time and attention. So go ahead and answer it. [I promise it's not a trick question.] Please spend a moment just thinking about why you date. Don't worry: Kerri and I aren't going to ask you to write anything down. This isn't a test.

As you probably know, people date for different reasons. Consider the answers I received when I posted this question on a non-Christian online forum:

- "I date for the enjoyment of being with somebody."
- "Sex; if you don't date, it's hard to get laid."

- "I know this sounds selfish, but if your date is hot, it can make all the difference when you're making an appearance. So I guess I am selfish."
- "I date because I'm hoping to find a husband, I suppose."
- "The female orgasm is a terrible thing to waste."

Isn't it nice that a basic question leads to some pretty basic answers? In addition to posting that question on a non-Christian website, I also posted it on a popular Christian forum. These are the answers I received:

- "*Hello?* I want to get married someday!"
- "If I ever hope to score a wife, I suppose I should practice dating, don't you think? That's what my mom told me."
- "Good question. I'm twenty-one, and, quite honestly, I date to have fun. That's kind of sad. But it's true. I always have something to do on Friday nights."
- "I date because I'm hoping God will show me who I am supposed to be married to."
- "My counselor thinks it's because I'm in love with being *in love.* She could be right."

If you'll notice, although the answers from the two websites might seem very different at first glance, the core need is the same. The answers all involve self-fulfillment. People tend to date to fill a void or need. But before you feel guilty, thinking I'm getting ready to yell at you for being so selfish, you should calm down a bit. Self-fulfillment is not necessarily a bad thing, especially when it comes to finding the love of your life. The companionship that's found between a man and a woman is something we need. I tend to believe it's a need that God infused into each of our emotional, spiritual, and physical DNA. In other words, God made us with a desire to seek out the fulfillment of male/female intimacy.

That's not to say that dating should always be about you. In fact, dating would probably be more fulfilling if you actually made it less about you. You're more than likely not new to the concept of pursuing a little selflessness. As people attempting to follow the teachings of Jesus, we should go into relationships thinking as much about the other person as we think about ourselves — if not more.

But in following the normal habits of human beings — to think about ourselves when it comes to dating — Kerri and I think it's only natural for us to write about you and how you date. Before we dive into section 1, you should first be aware of a few things:

- This book is split up into three sections: a section for both guys and girls, a section for guys, and a section for girls. Yes, I know it's a simple formula, but who needs complication?
- Reading this book will not result in your becoming an expert at dating. Nobody is an expert. As I said in the introduction, that's why there's an empire of Christian dating books! It sounds like we're not alone in our relational struggles.

- You will not relate to every issue we talk about in this book. And believe me, that's okay. In fact, I would feel free to consider that a very good thing.
- Truthfully, we kind of hope you don't relate to everything we mention in this book; that might mean the chances of your being relationally successful are pretty darn decent!
- Yes, we want you to be successful at dating, despite what the title suggests!

Let's get started.

FIRST THINGS FIRST:
GO AHEAD;
THINK YOU'RE NOT A PART OF THE PROBLEM!

It isn't that they can't see the solution.
It's that they can't see the problem.
G. K. CHESTERTON

Okay, guys and girls, here's the deal: One word that will probably get used more than a couple of times within the pages of this book is the word *issues*. That said, I (Kerri) actually hate the word. It's just difficult to get comfortable with, especially when they pertain to me. I guess being Christian doesn't make our issues any easier to admit.

YOUR QUESTION, OUR OPINION

[in the shape of an answer]

QUESTION:

I hate going to church now because all the older men are interested in me. In fact, this one guy keeps calling me after he got my number from a former friend of mine. I don't mean to be shallow, but am I supposed to date a man who is old enough to be my dad's younger brother just because he's a Christian? And why don't the guys my age ever ask me out? I thought church would be a good place to meet a nice guy, but it's just not happening as I planned.

Jessica, 23

ANSWER:

Dear Jessica,

I feel your pain, sister. I don't know why older guys want to date young girls and do things they did on dates in high school. I mean, come on; like you really want to walk hand in hand eating ice cream with some dude who is twice your age. Yuck! No offense, but men need to get a reality check and date women within their own age bracket. But, Jessica, don't give up on church. It's not God who is telling these guys to ask you out; that's got to be the Devil! Anyway, Jessica, stay strong, sister! The next time it happens, ask if he has a daughter your age and tell him he reminds you of your dad. That should do it.

Kerri

More than likely you have had the pleasure of knowing at least a couple of Christians who seem to be convinced they don't have any issues. Of course, you know otherwise. They do have issues; they'd just prefer to call them prayer requests instead. Big difference, huh? This reminds me that when I was little, my mama would say to me, "Kerri, talking about someone isn't considered gossip if your head is bowed!" I'm sure you know exactly what I'm talking about. Why is it we have such a hard time admitting that we don't have it all together? Unfortunately, this human flaw rears its ugly face most often when we're pursuing the opposite sex.

Oh, believe me, there was a time in my dating life when I became convinced that I didn't have any issues, that I was a perfect little angel. At the time, the only person who would have agreed with me was my Italian father. He believed wholeheartedly that if a man didn't instantly fall in love with his daughter, he must be gay. Whenever problems would arise in my relationships, I was *never* the one with the issue. It was always the guy's fault.

Yes, I was "that girl." Every time I got dumped I'd begin listing all the reasons my ex was the one who messed up. Honestly, I rarely considered the possibility that I might be a part of the problem or, at the very least, that I had really bad taste in men. [Of course, judging a potential mate in college consisted of asking which fraternity he belonged to, what his major was, and if he was from "old money." Even those snotty kids on *90210* weren't as ridiculous as I was.]

THE BEST DATING ADVICE I GOT

[personal advice from people in their twenties]

"This might seem silly, but I always keep floss in the glove compartment. You never know when it's going to come in handy — if you know what I mean." T.G., 28

[Thanks, T.G. We're pretty sure we know what you mean. Of course, I (Matthew) must admit I am a little frightened by the thought of how or when one would actually pull out the dental floss from the glove compartment and use it. But I do agree that while having a piece of leafy spinach between your two front teeth might not ruin your entire dating life, it won't help in scoring that good-bye kiss.]

"My advice is to pray. But not a prayer as in, 'God, bring me a husband.' I'm talking about 'God, continue to have mercy on me, for I am a big, fat ole mess' kind of praying." Keeandra, 25

"I got nothing." Geoff, 25

Of course, now that I look back on my dating life, I realize I had plenty of issues to spare, despite what my father wanted to believe. For example, I fell prey to the "Kerri Poppins" complex, otherwise known as the "I will save him" disease. That was one of my big issues when it came to dating. I always believed I could save the man with the big problem. Do you know how many stupid and silly mistakes I made because I refused to deal with my issue? Um, a lot! So often I'd date some emotionally stunted rebel who was mildly fascinated with my being a Christian, and I'd do my best to turn his entire life around in thirty days or less. Heck, my skills sometimes came with a money-back guarantee. To me, there was no guy out of reach. If he cried a lot, I'd tell myself it was romantic. Needless to say, I'd fall in and out of love with men who were manic-depressive just because I became addicted to the drama! Oh, I loved the drama. Eventually I learned that before I would ever have a snowball's chance in you know where of having a real relationship with the man of my dreams, I was going to have to admit that I was a part of the problem and find help.

> **FIVE "YOU" STATEMENTS THAT WILL RUIN YOUR DATING LIFE**
>
> 1. This is *your* fault — every bit of it.
> 2. I am angry because *you* made me get angry.
> 3. If this is going to work, *you* need to change.
> 4. *You* need an attitude adjustment.
> 5. Don't *you* dare put one bit of the blame on me.

If you want to ruin your dating life, continue to believe you're not a part of the problem.

Sometimes our issues seem so innocent and meaningless in regard to our relationships, but more often than not they're far from it. For instance, I bet that some of you reading this book are "mama's boys" or "daddy's girls," and when it comes to your relationships with the opposite sex, you're in search of a replacement for the kind of love and adoration you received from your mom or dad. That kind of issue might seem harmless to you, but to the one you're dating or *trying* to date, it feels like a gaping emotional hole that is impossible for him or her to fill.

So first things first: Do yourself a favor. Take an inventory of your own life instead of avoiding that "thing" you're thinking about right now — you know, the issue that's keeping you from getting involved emotionally or that's causing you to make horrible decisions in your relationships. Just like any good detox program, self-reflection is the first and most pivotal step.

I (Matthew) think Kerri makes an excellent point. More than likely when it comes to dating, you are your own worst enemy. Again, I know that sounds harsh, but it's usually very true. And you shouldn't be surprised. I mean, don't a lot of the issues we face come down to how *we* think, feel, and respond to a particular event or situation in our lives?

Before you get mad at me for blaming everything on you, make sure you haven't heard me incorrectly; I'm not suggesting you're the cause of *every* relationship problem that exists in your life. You could be, but I have no way of knowing that. For instance, I had a friend whose father developed a pretty severe problem with alcohol. Throughout most of my friend's teenage years, he became preoccupied with trying to help his dad, taking it upon himself to remind him to go to AA meetings or to pour out the liquor bottles when he found them underneath the bathroom sink. But instead of helping his dad, he actually became rather codependent upon his father's problem, which led to some major issues with trusting other people. In the end, my friend was not able to fix his dad's alcoholism, but he was able to change the way he thought about it and reacted to it. Also, it might be worth mentioning that for a long time, he seemed incapable of being able to see how his father's problem could ever affect his relationships with women. But of course it did. Whenever he dated, he always tried to fix his dates' issues but was never able to see his own.

So the moral of the story is this: We may not be the culprit for every relationship problem we've ever had, but we *are* capable of changing ourselves. You'll absolutely sabotage your relationships if you blame everyone but yourself. So let's all take a good look in the mirror. But don't exacerbate the problem by placing all the blame on yourself. Rather, focus on thinking and rethinking your relationships as they relate to *you*. [*Cue "The More You Know" jingle.*]

QUESTIONS TO CONSIDER:

- Do you think you are a part of your dating problems?
- In what ways do you mess up your own dating situation?
- What do you believe are your core issues with dating?

POLITICALLY CHALLENGED

When I (Matthew) was a little kid, my parents recounted story upon story about their über-romantic courtship. They made it sound almost magical. By the way they told of their experiences — jitterbug dances at the firehouse, Friday nights at

KERRI'S TOP TEN

[worst places to take a first date]

1. Your ex's wedding
2. Six-day church retreat — the couples-only premarital getaway
3. Monastery weekend with a full vow of silence
4. Your church youth group's latest rendition of *Chicago*
5. Your church senior citizen group's latest rendition of *Cats*
6. *Carman: The Champion* on ice
7. Your flag-dancing ministry recital with audience participation
8. The early-bird senior buffet at your grandma's retirement home [where all the food has been liquefied]
9. Bingo night at the Catholic church after Father Willie serves Communion
10. Christian "Rockaraoke Karaoke" [where you're the host]

the drive-in movie, sneaking a peck or two before saying good night — dating seemed harmless and, in fact, enjoyable, in a *Grease* sort of way.

So when I got to dating age — which for me was sixteen years old — I didn't fear asking a girl out on a date. But honestly, looking back now, I'm thinking maybe I should have been a little more fearful. When I was in eleventh grade, I asked a girl out for the first time. Her name was Diana. I took her to our church's annual God-Prom. [*Don't ask; the most exciting thing that happened at God-Prom was Scrabble.*] I thought everything about her was amazing. She loved God. She was pretty. She had bangs that nearly touched the ceiling — no, seriously, she was taller than me if you included her bangs. She smelled good. And her hands were the softest things I had ever touched, at least as far as I could remember. But two months into our little relationship — the day before Valentine's Day, in fact — she broke up with me. And the breaking up wasn't the worst part; it was the fact that almost everyone in my class knew about it before I did. That was horrible.

"What? She's breaking up with me?" I said to the guy who finally broke the news to me. "Oh my gosh! But then what was last night all about?"

"Last night? What happened last night? The two of you were at church," he countered.

"Yeah, but while everyone else was paying attention to the sermon, we were holding hands; it was the best hand holding I've ever experienced."

"I didn't see you guys holding hands, and I was sitting right next to you," he said.

"Come on, man; it was happening underneath my coat. We didn't want our parents to know what we were doing."

"Wow. Well, all I know is that she doesn't like you anymore. It just sucks that you're the last one to hear about it, man."

Maybe you know a little bit about what I felt. Whenever you began dating — whether it was in middle school or college or, because you were sheltered as a child, even after receiving your BA — one thing you probably learned soon after was this: There are politics in dating.

That word admittedly carries a negative connotation. But *politics* does not have to be a dirty word — at least not as dirty as we have made it out to be. It's simply how people handle, build, and establish relationships. Dating politics can involve choosing the right words to use when asking someone out, engaging in smart conversation with your prospect's parents, or deciding what stories to tell [and not to tell] at dinner.

Of course, *dirty* politics do creep their way into most relationships. And when they surface, dirty relationship politics ruin things quickly. And forgive me for harping on a previous point, but dirty politics in relationships with the opposite sex are usually displayed because of our own weaknesses. For example, things tend to go sour when we're trying to hide something. It's no different than a politician trying to hide his dirty little secrets — think Mark Foley. In other words, some of us might try to use dirty politics to hide an insecurity or something in our past or the fact that our feelings don't run quite as deep as we've made our dating prospect believe they do.

As you might suspect, though politics in relationships aren't stereotypically a masculine or feminine habit, the ways in which guys and girls politick can differ greatly. I've seen quite a few Christian guys play dirty by keeping a relationship with a girl vague. A guy might tell his SO (Significant Other) that his feelings are ambiguous only because he doesn't want to — and this is where he tries to quote Song of Solomon — "awaken love until God says it's time." And I'm quite sure that for some guys, the desire to be careful is a sincere one. But more often than not, a guy is being vague for one of these reasons:

   a. He's avoiding commitment to any one girl like it's the plague. [I'd compare his distaste for commitment to

the feelings he has toward a plague of flies. What can
I say? You cramp his style.]

b. He's in love with the idea of *being* with someone but
definitely not with being with *someone*. [He's a *playa*.]

c. He's totally up for the thrill of the chase but, um, not
so much the catch. [Yeah, and I'm comparing girls
to fish. Well, before you get upset, just remember *he*
started it.]

d. He's waiting to find out what another girl's true
feelings are, so he's balancing two ladies at once. [Hey,
if the thing with the other girl ends up not working
out, you might actually have a chance to play second
fiddle!]

Yeah, most guys play the "Politics of Vague," but only
Christian guys have the audacity to use Scripture to support
their behavior. And more than likely they end up making *you*
feel bad for questioning them.

But ladies, *puh-leeze*, you're hardly innocent in the game
of politics. In fact, you God-loving females, rather than using
ambiguity for your benefit, prefer the "Politics of Playing
Dumb" because you don't know how to be — or sometimes
seem incapable of being — honest. Oh, you're not familiar
with the playing-dumb scenario? *Yeah, right!* The "Politics of
Playing Dumb" is a tactic that's quite user friendly, meaning it
can be used in a number of situations. Christian women who
use this tactic best use it not only while displaying a smile that
impresses clergy but also with complete believability. Consider
the "Politics of Playing Dumb" as it is used in the following

scenario [this is only one situation; like I said, the POPD is *very* user friendly].

A certain Christian guy is pursuing you [for the purposes of this scenario, you are the generic Christian girl], but you are completely uninterested in him. Ladies, I know you know what I'm talking about. Instead of kindly letting the guy know that you're *just not that into him*, you play along as if you think he's just interested in being your friend. *You smile. You laugh. You even hug him when he walks into church.* But after three nondates, six coffee meetings at Starbucks, and one "unplanned" meeting with his parents, he decides it's finally time to reveal his heart: "I think I'm beginning to fall for you." At this juncture, what do you say? "What!?!?!?" you shriek. "You like me? You're not serious, are you? Oh, Brian, I didn't know you were interested in me like *that*. I thought you just wanted to be friends. Oh, this is embarrassing; well, the problem is, I'm kind of dating *Jesus* right now. Sorry." [And then you proceed to crush his little heart.]

It wouldn't have been so bad had you not asked him to help you move into your new apartment, fix a leaky faucet, put down your new hardwood floors, and zip up the hot little dress you wore out to Starbucks.

Here's another little example of how we use dirty politics in dating: the "Politics of Physical Guilt." Oh, yeah! This is a good one. It's a form of dirty politics that I have [for better or worse] perfected. [So don't do as I do; do as I say.] The "Politics of Physical Guilt" commonly occurs in scenarios such as the following.

Rose and Wally have been out on four dates. And guess

what? They totally dig each other. No, seriously; she thinks Wally's TMP (Total Marriage Potential) and he thinks Rose has assets King Solomon would use fruit to describe. And despite both of them being total Calvinists and consequently believing wholeheartedly in the total depravity of man [and woman], that hardly stops them from thinking they're about as close to nondepraved as two twentysomething Christian singles can become this side of eternity. Everything in their relationship is going just fabulous — that is, until the conclusion of their fifth date. On that date, Rose and Wally go out to Ruby Tuesday. He eats BBQ chicken wings. She settles on French onion soup. Afterward, they end up going back to her place to watch *Ugly Betty* and snuggle on the couch. Rose is still wearing a hot little red number she borrowed from her friend. Wally is wearing jeans and a Gap sweater. While the couple watches Betty go another sixty minutes without a makeover, Rose's left hand grows very familiar with Wally's upper body. Oh, it's nothing too hot, but certainly she is having a little fun exploring. Before long, they both begin to dive into the heat of the moment. Wally maneuvers his body to be able to kiss Rose head-on. Rose's body somehow falls into a sixty degree angle, a position that apparently has gotten her in trouble in the past. Wally's right hand begins playing Twister on Rose's body. Rose returns the favor. When the two have Twistered down to their skivvies, Wally says, "Oh, gosh, we can't be doing this." He leans back against the sofa and slowly begins putting his clothes back on. "I should go," he says with a defeated look on his face.

The next day, Rose calls Wally on her way to work just like she has for the last three weeks. But Wally doesn't answer. When

Rose gets to work, she sends Wally an e-mail. No response. She leaves another voice mail on his cell. Worried about Wally's well-being, Rose stops by his workplace during lunch. When she sees him, her first thought is, *Thank God he's all right*, but her second thought is, *Oh no, something's up.*

"Why haven't you returned my calls, Wally?" asks Rose.

"It's been a crazy morning," mumbles Wally unconvincingly.

"What's wrong?"

"Nothing."

"Yes, there's something wrong," she says, looking worried. "What is it?"

"We can talk about it later."

"No, let's talk about it now, hon."

After much coaxing, Wally finally offers, "I don't think we should see each other anymore. I can't do this any longer."

"What? Are you kidding me?" Rose's heart begins to beat faster. "Why are you saying this?"

"Because I feel like crap," he says. "Last night never should have happened."

"Oh, don't be silly, Wally; we made a mistake. We can work through this." Rose grabs hold of his hand, but Wally angrily pulls it away.

"I need some time alone."

"Wally, I really like you," says Rose, a tear rolling down her face.

"I've gotta go. I've got work to do."

Does this sound even vaguely familiar? Okay, other than the names Wally and Rose, does it sound familiar? Though real-life conversations are often more heated and emotional, I've known an awful lot of Christians who have lived through a situation where they felt so much guilt over one physical mishap that the only thing they could do was escape the relationship. In their quick exit, they usually failed to consider how their decision would affect their SO or the good thing they might be giving up or the fact that one mistake does not constitute a completely defunct relationship. All they could feel or see was the guilt their heart was experiencing at the moment, so they ended up saying things they didn't mean and doing some pretty stupid things that made the physical mishap seem almost harmless.

Dating Christians can be like dating time bombs; we come into someone's life with the best of intentions, but when we make one tiny error or when the person we're interested in screws up one thing, BOOM! it's over. So many of us look back at our past relationships and all we can see in our path is a massive amount of hurt, pain, and frustration and an unhealthy dose of psychotic behavior. And usually the dirty politics we play happen because we lack integrity, guts, honesty, kindness, or good people skills.

Some Very Basic Advice to Avoid Playing Dirty in Dating!

1. **Think before you speak.** Unless you're simply a mean-spirited person unable to take other people's feelings into consideration, most "political" situations can be avoided by simply *thinking* before talking. Don't make hasty decisions. If your decision is 100 percent

emotionally or physically based, it's usually the wrong decision.

2. **Beginning any breakup with the words, "God told me," is almost always unfair.** Pulling the Almighty into the politics of breaking up is pretty sketchy. There is, of course, the rare instance — like if you're Moses or King David — in which invoking the will of God upon somebody's life is acceptable. But usually, pulling the God-card during a breakup is a cop-out. I know telling someone your feelings for him or her have changed is very difficult, but it's the right thing to do. Blaming God is not!

3. **Don't become physically involved until your feelings are certain.** Okay, so I'm not talking about *knowing whether or not you're going to marry the person*, but as you know, it's very possible for you to be physically interested in a person without being emotionally, mentally, spiritually, or otherwise interested. And let's face it: The crazy part of this whole thing is that sometimes when things are heating up physically, your perspective about all the other areas of interest can become skewed. You might end up feeling emotionally and mentally connected when you're lip-locked, but those feelings are known to change or become skewed again — this time in a different way — when the heat wave has passed.

4. **Don't make up fake scenarios in hopes of forcing a person to break up with you.** You would be surprised at what people will do to get their significant others

to break up with them. Fake a death. Proclaim insanity. My friend Tom once told a girl that he was called to the mission field so she would leave him. He says it worked. But that's beside the point; despite tactics like these working, they're mean and manipulative.

5. **Work through your personal issues; don't let them mess up a good thing.** Now, when I say personal issues, I mean your insecurities, your mental issues, your spiritual faux pas, your tendencies to be co-dependent [we'll talk about that later] or angry [I think we'll talk about that later too], or your frustrations with family, career, and so forth — in other words, all the stuff that might be causing you to play dirty in the first place. Don't let these issues cause grief for your lover [*is it okay to say "lover" in a Christian book?*] or the person you hope to be your lover. Of course, even when we work through things, there's no guarantee that our loved ones won't still feel their stinging effects, but as long as you're attempting to work through them, at least you're not in denial that you have any issues. Be honest with yourself and also with the person you're dating. It's unfair to let your issues create unneeded drama in relationships.

6. **Be willing to talk.** Too often when we're in the middle of a frustrating season in life, instead of being willing to talk about our issues with our loved ones, we shut them out. Again, it's not fair to the other person for us to instantly shut down when a relationship gets difficult. I've seen so many people who in

the middle of a hard time in a relationship refuse to discuss the problem in a rational manner. Remember, being like Jesus means we are to seek humility, and sometimes humility requires us to open up and reveal what's going on inside. Which brings me to my last point.

7. **Above all, pursue humility and kindness.** Even the most difficult conversations can be greatly helped just by being humble and applying a little kindness. Ever heard the phrase, "You win more with honey than with vinegar"? It's true! Every relationship you build, regardless of whether or not you're meant to be married, is a chance to serve someone else.

 QUESTIONS TO CONSIDER:

- I've certainly not listed all the political games that people play in relationships. Name some other kinds of "yuck" that you believe Christians bring into relationships.
- Take a look in the mirror; what relational politics do you play? Be honest with yourself. Hey, if you're really in the mood for an evaluation, consider getting one of your exes to answer this question for you!
- Have you ever been hurt by dating politics? If so, how did that experience affect your future relationships?

OVERSPIRITUALIZING:
THE WRECKING BALL TO YOUR SOCIAL LIFE

If you've been a Christian for a little bit of time, you know that when it comes to the topic of dating, Christians have a various array of thoughts about how God weaves himself [or his story] into the relationship picture. Some Christians believe that God is all about weaving every part of himself into our relationships. These Christians have every confidence and faith that God has indeed chosen one specific person for them to marry. Which must mean that in King Solomon's case, God chose seven hundred specific women for him to experience until death did *all of them* part. These Christians also tend to believe that God commands a specific manner in which to pursue a marriage relationship.

But not every Christian thinks that God is so intertwined in romance. Quite a few Christians believe that God simply desires us to find a good person, which could be anybody of the opposite sex who has a relationship with Jesus. They believe that upon marrying this good Jesus-loving person, their ultimate responsibility as a couple is to pursue serving him and his kingdom together.

And there are still other Christians who wonder if God plays any significant role at all in the story of love. Of course, some of us combine these three perspectives in our dating philosophies, and I'm sure there are many Christians whose idea of God's role in relationships wouldn't mirror *any* of these three points. But I'm not going to try to prove which role God *actually* plays; much like any big theological debate within Christianity today — such as speaking in tongues, predestination, or the gifts of the Spirit — all of these theories can be validly supported with Scripture, at least to some extent. And as the case usually is, those who might oppose any of these views can often use Scripture to support their thinking too.

Since I'm not going to bore you with my opinion about this debate, you might be wondering why I went to the trouble of writing about these three perspectives. Well, my point is to demonstrate just how much thought and energy Christians put into discovering God's role in dating. But sometimes in the process of trying to figure out God's place, we end up over-spiritualizing things, and when we do that, we risk missing key opportunities [like meeting our future spouses].

If you're not familiar with the art of overspiritualizing relationships, consider the rules overspiritualizers follow.

First of all, consume lots of time fretting, arguing over, and contemplating theological differences as they relate to dating. I know this routine well. It was once my finest talent to take biblical passages out of context and relate them to why I was still single. Consequently, right out of college I was tempted to believe that I was one of the individuals God had chosen to be gifted with the blessing of celibate living [*um, yeah, that didn't last very long*]. But I had come to that conclusion because I had turned twenty-three and I was still single and convinced I had no hope in sight — and God knows there are a lot of Christians out there who get hitched somewhere between puberty and college graduation for this very reason [*not that there's anything wrong with that!*]. But in addition to almost everyone in my church believing I was either (a) an old man, (b) incompatible, or (c) *gay*, it didn't help that I had just read in the Bible where the apostle Paul implies that it is actually best for Christians if they choose not to marry. I think the exact quote is something like, "Marriage sucks! You should be like me, the great apostle Paul! However, if you're *constantly* in need of cold showers, then I guess you can settle down with a good woman."

Okay, that brings me to my second point: If you're really hoping to overspiritualize like a pro, please, by all means, go out of your way to equate your dating life to the lives of famous biblical couples. It's a ton of good fun! If you're going to learn how to date, why not learn from the finest daters in history? Learn what it means to be truly intimate with the opposite sex by comparing and contrasting your personal love story with the love story of Adam and Eve [*Don't be tempted by silly but dangerous snakes!*], Abraham and Sarah [*If all else fails, tell people your girlfriend is actually your sister*], and, of course, Jacob and Rachel [*Work hard for seven years. Get tricked into marrying your significant other's homelier sibling. Then be manipulated by the father of said wife to work seven more years so you can marry the true love of your life*]. See? Isn't this fun? The true lesson here: Not every biblical love story is relevant to your dating life.

Lastly, invent lots of biblically based theories about your dating life. This is much easier than it might sound. If you're a beginner, you can do this by making the following statements the next time you're in your sassy singles' Sunday school class:

- "I'm just waiting on God to bring me the man [or woman] I need." [*This one also works great when you're in small groups.*]
- "I think I'm supposed to be dating Jesus right now."

[*Yes! I hear he's very nice.*] We'll be covering this one more later on in the book!

- "God couldn't care less that I'm single!" [*This might be true, but when you say this one, you'll learn that it comes with bonus gifts: lots of pity from other single people and at least one blind date.*]

Okay, wait just a minute; you did get the point of all that, right? [Please don't take offense to that question. To some Christians, using sarcasm to shed light on a situation is almost as effective as a movie about America starring Hugh Grant.] Anyway, hopefully you got the point! Of course, you probably think that some parts of my "how to overspiritualize" examples are ridiculously exaggerated. Well, maybe they are exaggerated. But that doesn't negate the fact that an unhealthy mind-set toward God and relationships [and when I say unhealthy mind-set, I mean that of a person who thinks God takes time out of his busy schedule to date humans] will make your dating life unnecessarily difficult.

Two Big Questions [and Short Answers] People Ask About God and Dating

1. **Does the Bible give us advice specifically about dating?** Surprisingly, the Bible doesn't give specific advice about dating. Now, before you get worked up, some scholars think King Solomon's Song of Solomon gives good advice about romancing the opposite sex;

however, others think SOS is simply a king's poem describing his longing for romance and that the characters in the story are fictional, as in a *wish* for what true romance could be. Regardless of how you read SOS, though the love story is passionate and sensual and *good* in the eyes of God, it certainly doesn't give us a step-by-step plan for good dating. I mean, like I wrote earlier, King Solomon had seven hundred wives, which meant he was either an expert at wooing the ladies *or* he was a rather awful husband. Of course, in addition to Solomon's poetry, the Old Testament is full of stories of men and women getting married. But let's face it: Though we can definitely glean wisdom from the personalities, attributes, and words of the men and women of the OT — which can be helpful in certain aspects of dating — it's difficult for us in the twenty-first century to relate to their actual relational practices, especially considering they didn't really *date.*

2. **So when it comes to dating, is the Bible irrelevant?** Absolutely not! The Bible might not mention dating by name, but as you know, the Bible does teach us how to live and how we should treat other people. Again, it comes back to "me," which is a good thing, since you can change only how you do things. And even though the Bible doesn't give much specific advice about the art of coupling, the writers of the Bible certainly spent a great deal of time teaching us how God would want us to live as individuals, which includes such attributes as purity of heart, love and kindness, peacefulness,

humility, grace, passion, integrity, honesty, compassion, servanthood, confidence, and prayer. As you probably know, all of these attributes make very good habits within the context of dating. Sure, they're not easy to live, but they are good habits to practice.

When It Comes to God and Dating, You Might Take These Three Ideas into Consideration

[they're not laws or anything,
just a little common sense and maybe a hint of sarcasm]

1. **Not every dating problem is a spiritual one.** Yes, by all means, pray as often as you would like to for God to bring you a spouse. And, of course, it's fine if you want to attend Wednesday-night services just in case your aunt Milly's pool boy shows up. And I guess it isn't too terribly unhealthy for you to think God is punishing your dating life because he's putting part of the blame for global warming on you. But eventually you might have to realize that instead of your dating issues being spiritual in nature, it may be that you just need to work out, not be so needy, or find a *real* job that pays more than $1.50 above minimum wage. When I put it that way, it would be much simpler if your dating issues were spiritual ones, in that they wouldn't require a treadmill. Because who likes a treadmill?

2. **God doesn't usually play matchmaker.** Yes, the Bible teaches that on occasion he helped unite a man and woman, but that certainly doesn't mean we should sit around and wait for him to drop the person of our dreams into our lives. Feel more than free to ask God for wisdom in helping you discover what might be his plan for your life, but if you sit back and just wait for God to magically give you a spouse, it's not likely going to happen. So get on that treadmill and go meet some people!

3. **Don't be a spiritual snob.** One of my biggest pet peeves when I was dating was Christians who pretended to be on a higher spiritual plane than everyone else. I struggled to believe that even *God* could sit in the room with them for more than fifteen minutes — they were *that* annoying. Of course, spiritual snobs are rather harmless creatures when you just want to be friends, but look out; they're awful to date because they usually see themselves as spiritual thermometers for all things relational.

Here's the bottom line: Don't try to make every aspect of dating into a spiritual proclamation to all who are around you. In the end, nobody cares whether you revealed how godly you were by following the dating path of Ruth and Boaz or you ended up finally caving in to the pressure and found the love of your life online at eHarmony.com. Stop using God as a way to complicate your dating life. Yes, I said complicate. I realize that most people attempt to bring God into the dating picture to make things easier, but because *you're* the one bringing God into the picture [and not letting him enter the picture on his own free will], more often than not — because you are a human being and cannot manifest God whenever you want — you're going to eventually complicate your dating life. And you know what the really sad part is? One day, when you realize that your dating life is on a very rocky road, you'll tell somebody, "Yeah, God has really been working on me the last few years; I guess he wants me to be single."

If you want God to become a part of your dating life, here's a thought: Invite him. If he shows up, say thank you. But whatever you do — and this is more often a problem for girls — do not, under any circumstances, ask him out. I mean it, girls; don't do it. Get some guts and tell the guy you're dating that you've lost interest. Or admit that you simply can't get a date. Don't pretend God wants to date you for a while.

 ## QUESTIONS TO CONSIDER:

- How do you think God interacts with us when it comes to dating? Do you believe he has one special person chosen for you? Or do you believe you could fall in love with anybody of the opposite sex who is Christian?
- What stories in the Bible have encouraged you to pursue godly relationships?
- If God were teaching a class on dating, what do you think he would teach?

BE OUR GUEST: KISS DATING GOOD-BYE!
[BUT FYI: THE REPERCUSSIONS CAN STINK!]

Air power is an unusually seductive form of military
strength, in part because, like modern courtship, it
appears to offer gratification without commitment.

ELIOT COHEN

Speaking of God and, more specifically, of our habit toward
overspiritualizing the process of dating, I figure we should get
this little *kissing* issue out of the way toward the beginning of
the book.

As you probably know, back in the late 1990s a little book
called *I Kissed Dating Goodbye*, by Joshua Harris, sold a ton of
copies and helped spread the word about how much fun courting [*not* dating] could be! Despite sounding like something that
might have last happened on the *Mayflower*, courting became the
topic of a lot of evangelicals' conversations. It was seen as wise
and even as a mistake-free approach to finding a spouse. Youth
pastors had their youth groups read it, hoping their church kids
would run from dating. Rebecca St. James preached from it
during her concerts. In fact, a lot of Christian celebrity singles
became part of a big marketing force behind Joshua's book.

I remember all too well when the book came out. It seemed
as though everyone was asking the big question, "So are you two
dating or courting?" It was a fine, if simple, message, but due
to the passion in Joshua's delivery combined with the cultish

audience response, this book became the dating Bible, spreading the good news: Don't date at all and you'll find a spouse sooner than ever! Eventually, readers began to realize that Joshua's story [the one in which he gets married to the woman of his dreams by age twenty-one] is not necessarily a story that comes true for everyone. Today, kissing dating good-bye is not as popular as it was in the nineties and early twenty-first century, but it does still have quite a following.

Now that he's a bit older and I can only imagine wiser, Joshua probably has reconsidered some of the content in *Kissing*. Though I must admit, some of the points he makes are valid. Joshua is right when he says that we are too self-centered. He's also correct when he suggests that people struggle knowing where the line of premarital intimacy should be drawn. And, yes, teenagers get *way* too serious sometimes. But my beef with the book is this: Just because we're flawed individuals — you know, people who can pretty much mess up a variety of good things — that hardly means we should throw out the entire concept of dating.

There are a good number of problems with Joshua's theory; I'm certainly not going to list them all here. That would be like taking out a machine gun, and because I know that quite a few people *loved* that book and found a lot of wisdom in it, I will refrain from an all-out war. But that's not to say I'm not going to throw a couple of darts. One of the problems with Joshua's theory could be this: A lot has changed about our culture — for good and for bad — since the year 1845. [*In all fairness, Joshua doesn't mention 1845 in his book; I'm simply using it to make a point.*] And, truthfully, I think it's almost impossible to take one concept out of an era or time frame and apply it to how we do things today unless a good portion of our personal culture aligns with it too. In other words, let's say you've decided you want to pursue your lifelong partnership with the opposite sex by courting. [*Okay, hold that thought for a moment.*]

For those of you who are rather clueless as to what courting entails, here's a very short definition, one that should not be used as a summary of what Joshua thinks about dating [*that would be unfair to him and to you*], but one that will give you a basic idea:

> **court·ship** *n*: The act or period of wooing a woman* [Is it just me, or is *woo* a funny word? Does anyone ever say, "Hey, bro, let's head out to the party and see if we can woo some ladies?" And, ladies, do you want us guys to ask for your permission before we begin to woo? Or should we ask your father? Wooing is complicated.]

In addition to that fine definition of courting, according to the website Courting.org — yes, there's a courting site online for your enjoyment — there are four ingredients to proper courting:

1. **Action — what to do first.** [This is the guy's job! Ladies, please stand perfectly still. I'd truly hate for your bonnet to get wrinkled.]

---

* *American Heritage Dictionary*, 1981, s.v. "courtship."

2. **Time frame — when to do it.** [Yeah, it's the guy's job
to keep track of this, too! Wait by the phone, ladies;
he'll call. No, I promise he will.]

3. **Pursuance — will it become a habit?** [Um, yeah, the
guy does this too. In fact, I think this might be the
wooing part.]

4. **Response of a woman — what does she think?**
[Ladies, finally you get a say!]

Yeah, and just in case you didn't know this one, Joshua Harris
is a guy. And, um, he wrote the book.

Okay, so back to why it might be problematic for you to
become successful at finding your mate the "courting" way. If
we lived back in 1845, I would imagine those four ingredients
would have been pretty commonplace among social gatherings.
You know, back then a man would see a woman hanging out
next to her horse and carriage and think to himself, *She's hot.*
Or maybe he would think, *She looks quite dashing.* But, you see,
the difference for the guy from the year 1845 is this: He didn't
have to think about putting into practice the "rules" of courtship. He'd been taught since he was in grade school that talking
to the dashing girl's father would be the proper thing to do. In
other words, the rules were a natural part of his life. However,
can you imagine what would have happened if someone had
written a book in 1844 called *I Kissed Courting Goodbye* and
proposed going back to the Old Testament way of finding a
spouse? What if the young man would have tried to follow it?
I'm not sure, but it seems it would have caused quite the scene
if he were to have shown up with thirty-two goats and tried

to trade those goats with the girl's father in exchange for the daughter's hand in marriage.

Sure, that's a strange example to even imagine, but think about this: Applying the concept of courting to our twenty-first-century way of living might be just as extreme. Although it might be charming to certain conservative Christians, it's still pretty darn impractical in today's culture, primarily for these reasons:

1. Most fathers wouldn't know what to say to the young man who approached him for permission to date his daughter. In fact, he might think the guy is kind of odd.
2. The young woman might take offense to the fact that the boy isn't simply asking her out. Call me crazy, but she is capable of thinking for herself.
3. It allows "something" — which isn't dating but sure looks a lot like it — to occur between two people, and that "something" is vague and undefined.
4. In 1845, the activities that happened within a community were more conducive to the concept of courtship.

But while I think these are good reasons to not kiss dating good-bye, they're hardly the main reasons. Consider the following:

1. **You might be seen as kind of selfish.** I don't believe that a person who "kisses off" dating is being purposefully selfish; however, the Christians I know who have

tried it many times refused to date [or court] anyone who didn't fall in line with how they did things. I've seen a lot of good guys and girls turn away other good guys and girls just because one of them was unwilling to court or was uncomfortable with group dates or thought the idea of having a mentoring couple was odd. Not every person is fit for courtship, which brings me to my next point.

2. **You might not have the right personality.** For Joshua, courting might have been the best thing. But, you see, not every personality type is designed for following the rigid rules of courtship. Some people actually like a little "story" with their relationships. Now, proponents of courting might say, "But that story gets ugly sometimes." And they're absolutely right — it does get ugly. But trust me, so does courting.

So, yeah, don't hug, kick, curse, or kiss dating good-bye. Kissing it good-bye might only complicate things for you. Sure, if you're struggling in your dating life [like finding yourself incapable of being unattached even when you know your relationships are not healthy, or dating only for the physical benefits], you might take a break in order to get yourself healthy, but kissing the whole concept good-bye is usually not the answer. Truthfully, you'll more than likely just try to *woo* it back in a few days anyway. Or sleep with it. And that's not going to help anything.

QUESTIONS TO CONSIDER:

- Have you ever kissed dating good-bye? If so, were you successful at it? What was your experience?
- Is there any part of courting that intrigues you? If so, what part?
- Do you think courting promotes healthy relationships?

THINGS YOU CAN DO ON THE FIRST DATE TO RUIN YOUR DATING LIFE!

- Be noticeably anxious about the date. [Sweaty hands get extra credit!]

- Divulge your entire life story; believe me, your date totally wants to hear it. [Story about "secret crime" wins bonus points!]

- Talk too much and never let your date get a word in. Nothing is sexier.

- Drink way too much. Nothing is more attractive than having to be the designated driver on a first date. [Well, designated *backseat* driver might be a little better.]

- Smother your date; I bet he or she would love that.

WANT TO RUIN YOUR DATING LIFE?
BE NEEDY!

When I (Kerri) was growing up and learning about boys, one thing was certain: My mom did not want me to be needy. In other words, my Southern belle of a mother told me, "Don't call boys! It's not ladylike." I don't think she would have been too thrilled if she had seen me pin down Brandon Duck on the playground in kindergarten and make him tell me he loved me. He later dumped me for Jennie Grabda, and to this day, I think it was only because she was tan. But in a way, Mom was right. She wanted the young gentleman callers to pursue me in that old-fashioned style to prove that they really liked me. Is that so wrong? I don't think so. There is a dance to dating, one that God created. In my opinion, we need to learn how to do the dance with our dating partners and not try to speed up the pace.

Sadly, I didn't follow Mom's instructions. I'm a type A personality, and I always hated waiting. So instead of giving any male suitor a chance to actually pursue me, I jumped in with both feet. It was really attractive when I called one guy and said, "Hey, I just happen to be in your neighborhood. Want to hang out?" It never was the way to go, but I wasn't willing to wait on any man or even God for my relationships to naturally blossom. You know what? That's dangerous, like Ice from *Top Gun* dangerous! By being too needy, I was endangering the possibility of my having any chance of a real relationship. If you're needy, you're likely willing to compromise your standards, and the next thing you know, you're dating some person who's totally wrong for you. Or even worse, you end up marrying the person.

When you're feeling needy [and we've all been there], it's hard to control yourself. I know it sounds cheesy, but consider getting an accountability friend if you need one. When you feel like you're about to do something totally out of line, call this person and beg him or her to talk you out of it. I think we all need guidance in the dating jungle. Having like-minded friends is invaluable because they can be objective when you can't. They can be the ones to tell you that sending your SO a wedding cake with pictures of the two of you on it after the second date won't be as romantic as it seems in your head. Trust me, sometimes trying to be cute comes off as "stalker."

I (Matthew) agree with Kerri. Neediness might be one of the most unattractive qualities that a human being — male or female — can possess. When we're needy, we're basically screaming to the world, "I'm not satisfied in my own skin." In our efforts to fill that void and become satisfied [or to just feel comfortable], we end up making fools out of ourselves. And like Kerri suggested, those efforts can show up in a variety of traits. Take a look at the following list and see if any of these sound familiar to you. If you're not sure, get your best friend or one of your parents to be frank with you and give you his or her honest opinion about your *needy* factor.

You Might Be Seriously Needy If:

- You're codependent or need someone else's approval to be happy.
- You're self-centered, always fishing for a compliment.

- You're obnoxious, always making a fool out of yourself for the attention of others.
- You keep calling despite no returned calls.
- You have to be in a relationship.
- You get jealous easily.
- Your emotional well-being is based on whether or not you're dating.

KERRI'S IDEAS TO GET OFF THE DESPERATE TRAIN

1. **Pray to be patient.** Pray for God's will to be done even if it means a particular person won't be "the one." If you're serious about finding the right mate for you, you should not waste time on the runners-up.

2. **Think before you act.** If you think you have a history of doing things to scare off potential dates, be a little more careful this time. If you want to send a girl a gift, make sure it's appropriate for the situation and also for the amount of time you've been together. For example, after a couple of dates it's lovely to send some flowers with a note saying, "I had a great time last night. Look forward to seeing you soon." It's not okay to send a potted plant with a note saying, "We're planting our new life! Love you!"

3. **Realize you are valuable.** You deserve someone who is just as crazy about you as you are about him or her. You are a wonderful catch. Take some time to think about all you have to offer your future dates. Maybe it's

your great sense of humor or your kind heart. When your self-esteem is high, it makes it easier not to act in a needy or desperate fashion.

 ## QUESTIONS TO CONSIDER:

- What do you think others see as needy in your personality? Do you think they consider you a needy person?
- How can you stop being needy? Therapy? Prayer? Maturity?
- In your opinion, is being needy a sin?
- To some extent we are all needy. Do you believe this is a true statement?

A FEW SIMPLE RULES REGARDING CHRISTIAN SINGLES' GROUPS

Okay, so if you happen to find yourself joining a church singles' group, do yourself a big favor and follow these rules. Please do this. I (Matthew) promise that the very essence of your dating career depends on it.

- **It's not a hookup joint.** That's not to say *dating* won't happen — and it would actually be awesome if it happened more often — but if you join a Christian singles' group with the motive of hooking up, may the fake gods of unwanted celibacy fall upon you for many moons. [*No, I'm not New Age.*]

- **Resist the temptation to make the group your only friends.** Sure, they're nice people, but you'll need a little more cultural influence than just them! Trust me, I know that so-and-so's a nice girl, but if you don't want to be the next forty-five-year-old single to be spearheading your yearly Unmarried Servants' Fall Retreat, I suggest you keep your singles' group attendance on a very tight leash. Or you know that Sheila will be nominating you to replace her when she turns forty-five.

- **If your singles' group is known by an acronym, leave immediately.** I'm not trying to make you a stuck-up jerk, but come on, you've got a reputation to protect, and attending the FLOCK — Females Living Out Christ's Kingdom — is only making that more difficult!

- **Keep it to one activity a week [maybe two, but only if they're mission related].** Just trust me on this one, all right?

- **If you're a male over the age of thirty and you attend a church singles' group that's mostly female and under the age of twenty-three, I hate to break it to you, but everybody thinks you're creepy.** And if you have a mustache or goatee, multiply that creepiness times ten.

- **If upon joining a church singles' group the word *single* becomes about as tolerable as the words *moist*, *sack*, or *pianist*, you might want to find a new church.** Believe it or not, *single* isn't a dirty word.

- **No making out on missions trips.** You know when the music fades, so will the relationship.

REMAINING STAGNANT:
THE BEST WAY TO HALT SELF-IMPROVEMENT

Can I (Matthew) brag for a moment? Not about myself, of course; that would be downright obnoxious. But I'd like to take a moment to boast a little proudly [in a cute husband sort of way] about my wife. I promise not to get too over the top, but what can I say? She just impresses me so much.

So on top of the fact that my wife is smart, she's creative, she's giving, she's business savvy, and she looks great in a dress that's just a little too tight. Now, I'm not trying to suggest she's perfect, but she does certainly leave me wowed most of the time. When people meet Jessica, one way they tend to describe her is "always together." Considering that I have ADHD, I'm a total creative, and I struggle at times with being a little too fond of myself, the quality of being "always together" fascinates me. Of course, I have ADHD, and anything that moves, makes noise, or sparkles [excluding sequins] fascinates me. But despite *me*, Jessica takes great pride in living her life in a way that she's constantly being challenged, learning new things, and meeting new people. That might very well be one of the sexiest qualities about Jessica: the desire to take life by the horns and experience it to the fullest, to never stop learning things that better her and make her feel better about herself. That quality is just one of the reasons I pursued her; she's a go-getter, always ready to jump into something new and exciting. Okay, I'll stop bragging now. I don't want to make you nauseous.

But that quality of not being stagnant in life is definitely a quality a lot of people lack. It's honestly depressing sometimes to meet people who say, "My life is going nowhere," but seemingly do nothing to change their situations. But it's not only depressing to watch; it's also unattractive. I mean, it's not like they have to possess the drive of Oprah, but come on, they could push themselves a little. A little growth wouldn't hurt them, that's for sure. People who are consistently looking for ways to grow are more attractive than those who are satisfied with the status quo, especially when the status quo is less than the best that God has for them.

Now, some of you don't need to hear this advice. You're the kind of people who are constantly looking for ways to better yourselves or keep from becoming bored with life. But a lot of Christian singles get stuck in a routine by the time they turn twenty-seven and don't realize they're in that routine until they're thirty-four and disgusted with their lives.

And again, it's frustrating to watch. Whenever I meet people in their late twenties or early thirties who desire to be married but aren't having the best of luck scoring any quality time with decent candidates [i.e., dates], one of the first things I want to know is whether or not they are doing things to make themselves better. Are they furthering their education? Do they have hobbies, new or old? Do they look for opportunities to step out of their comfort zones and take risks? Do they travel or go on missions trips? Do they take care of themselves or at least attempt to? Do they try to make the most of their lives?

That said, I can't tell you how many Christian singles I meet who regularly retell their story about *still* being single. Nice Christian women everywhere complain about never getting asked out, and good Christian guys voice their frustrations about being turned down. But then, and I know this might seem a little harsh, too often when they reveal the rest of their story — the dead-end job or the lack of concern for their health or the hours of daytime television they consume on a daily basis or the fact that they have no hobbies or interests — a part of me realizes *why* they're still single, why people are not all that excited about spending an evening with them one-on-one. I know some people say, "There's no reason *why* you're single; it's just not God's *time* for you yet." And while in many cases I agree with such an argument, I can't help but wonder if God's waiting on them to get off their lazy butts and do something with their lives.

Does growth guarantee success in dating? No, of course it doesn't, but it always helps the cause. Most people aren't interested in spending the rest of their lives with someone who isn't interested in something or going somewhere or pursuing life with a little gusto. So be frank with yourself and consider the following questions:

- Do you have a hobby? When was the last time you enjoyed your favorite pastime?
- When was the last time you learned how to do something new?
- Do you ever do anything that truly challenges you?
- Could you put a little more time and attention toward your appearance? I'm not talking about being a diva; I mean just taking care of what you've got.
- Would going back to school help you better your life?
- Are you culturally aware?

- Have you ever considered volunteering at church or for a local charity?

These are simple questions, but they're relatively important, especially as they relate to your dating life. When you're out doing stuff that makes you a better person, it's a sign of confidence and security, and it's healthy and attractive.

 ## QUESTIONS TO CONSIDER:

- Would you date or marry someone with a dead-end job?
- Wouldn't you feel good if the person you were dating shared one of your interests? Like history, culture, art, or soccer?
- Do you think a person's lack of growth reveals laziness? Would you date a lazy person?
- Does learning new things interest you?
- Do you like seeing other people enjoying themselves?
- Is furthering oneself a godly trait?

JUST A FEW IDEAS FOR GROWING YOU!

[well, you won't get taller, but life might become a little richer]

- **Go back to school.** With high-speed Internet, it's easier now than ever to further your education, even if you live in the middle of nowhere! You might not be interested in getting a four-year degree or your master's, but you can take a class on a topic that interests you — maybe a course on religion, politics, or a trade that could possibly help you in your career.

- **Learn a new trade or hobby.** Learn how to sew, scrapbook, cook, wood carve, fix a car, design a computer program — anything that might become a hobby or help you in your job.

- **Volunteer.** Whatever the cause, helping a community, ministry, nonprofit organization, hospital, or any type of charitable organization is a great growth opportunity and a good way to meet new people.

- **Get sporty.** In other words, join some kind of community sports league. Not only is it fun, but it's also a good way to get a little exercise.

- **Once in a while, do something cultural.** Go to a special art exhibit, the theater, a lecture — something you wouldn't ordinarily do.

- **Stay current on current events.** You'd be surprised how many people are out of touch with the news. You don't have to go crazy, but it wouldn't hurt for you to stay a little informed.

Of course, there are countless ways to better yourself, and I can't list them all right here, so I'll let you be a little creative.

BEING SHALLOW

[IT'S NOT JUST FOR WATER]

Men, I (Kerri) don't want you to think this part on being shallow is just for women, because all of us do it. You know how it is: We don't judge a book only by its cover [though that might be one of our *biggest* faults]. We also judge a book by who else is reading it and how popular it is on Amazon.com before we even open it up. Why do you think Amazon posts all those reader reviews? I'm sure if there were a website that gave reviews for potential dates, it would be very popular. [Actually, I wouldn't be surprised if one of those sites actually exists.] You know, this is exactly what we humans have been doing for centuries in our relationships. Why do you think the Internet is so popular? You can decide if you want to date someone based on his or her picture, height, weight, and even income level. Hello! Could it get any easier?

But wait just a minute; how is the shallow approach really working for you? Well, let me be honest. For me, it sucked! I've always been known as the most shallow of my friends because they had a three-date rule to see if it was going to work out or not. They would go on three dates, and if there was no chemistry after that, they figured at least they gave it a good try [and they got free dinner]. However, that method didn't work for me. I didn't want to waste my time, so I had the thirty-second rule. If I couldn't see myself romantically involved [making out] with a guy in the first thirty seconds, I knew we didn't have "it." So why sit through another lame dinner at the Macaroni Grill?

I think it's important for all of us to remember that being shallow isn't just about looks. For instance, I remember going out with Rex, a guy I met on the Internet. He was HOT [a fireman] and a great dresser with sparkling green eyes. When he came to my door he looked exactly like his pictures, but when we started talking I just knew this date was going to be very long. Even though I was getting free sushi, it wasn't going to be worth it. I can't tell you why I didn't click with Rex. He was nice, but he wasn't impressive to me, so I promptly ended our date after dinner and a thirty-minute obligatory walk on the beach. I came home that night distraught, wondering what was wrong with me and why I was never satisfied. Now, truth be told, Rex just didn't have a personality that clicked with mine. I'm a comedian and I need someone with a dry, quick, and dark sense of humor to hold my attention. That's my own issue, I know. I suffered many boring dates looking for a Matt Damon look-alike with a Woody Allen sense of humor. It was a painful experience at times because I felt I would never meet someone who measured up to my standards.

But here is the deal: I decided to try to break my shallowness by going out with Grant, another guy I met on the Internet. On paper he looked good. Off paper he looked good too. He was in real estate and drove race cars and had six-pack abs. But once again I was falling asleep on our third and final date. My friends begged me to keep going out with him. They said he would grow on me. They said goose bumps are overrated. I gave it three shots and I was still bored to tears. We didn't have much in common except that we were both Christians. I convinced myself I'd definitely have to settle. I thought to myself, *Well, who cares if he's not funny? He's got a job and he's good-looking. Just settle and try to be happy.* But the irony is that with Grant, I was still totally being shallow by allowing myself to keep dating him because of his good job and nice hair. I thought, *At least he'll look good at parties!*

The next morning, I left for Ohio on a plane with some other comics to do a TV show. A friend of mine sat next to me and brought Krispy Kreme Doughnuts. We were laughing and having the best time, but of course he wasn't my type. We were friends. I had a definite rule never to date a friend. He also didn't have a car. And I wanted someone who at least had health insurance. *Pleeeeeeeaaase!*

Long story short, this guy was totally in love with God, and I started to see him in a different light. I asked him, "What do you want in a woman?" He said, "I want a girl with caller ID who still takes my calls!" All of a sudden everything about this guy looked attractive to me. Was he my type? No way. His idea of high fashion was Kmart. But God had plans for us, and I fell madly in love with him that day. I fell in love with his black socks and dirty tennis shoes, his Hawaiian shirts from 1998, every single detail about him. I loved his smile and his beautiful green eyes and the fact that he went out of his way to be a total gentleman to me at all times.

I couldn't have predicted that this crazy, broke comic would be the man of my dreams. God had to trap us both on an airplane to Ohio to make us realize it. That weekend God showed me how completely sexy it is to be with a man who prays and eats Krispy Kremes, Nestlé Toll House cookies, Auntie Anne's pretzels, and Chinese food all in one afternoon. I fell for Ron, who is now my husband, because God took the superficial blinders off my eyes so I could see how perfect he was for me. I wasn't his type either. He's Korean, so he wanted a long-legged Asian schoolteacher with benefits [health insurance, 401k, and so on]. He even said, "I'll never date a comic!" Ha! I guess I took that as a challenge and married him to prove him wrong. But the thing is that we both had been open to finally seeing what God had for us.

My relationship with Ron was truly the first relationship in my life that was different from all the others from the very beginning. My friends and family noticed that we were like two peas in a pod almost immediately, and two comedians getting together could only be an act of God. I found out immediately [once I convinced him to ask me out] that this crazy friend was everything I ever wanted in a guy and more. I just couldn't see it before. But this is the most important point: I didn't settle. Not one bit. God had bigger and better plans for my marriage, and I thank God I waited. I see now that God had all these plans for us to work together, travel together, make people laugh together. And if I had married an accountant with a big 401k plan, I don't think he would have quite understood why his wife was running around the country involved in a business that is 98 percent male and dinner wasn't on his table every night at six o'clock.

My pastor used to say, and I always hated hearing it, "You have to be the right person and stop looking for the right person." I was like, "Nice. Pastor, you have a wife and three kids and a house! How do you know what it's like for the rest of us out here?" But for me I think it was more like I had to be the right person so I could see the right person. [Hey, that rhymes!] He had been right next to me all along.

So I guess the moral of this little story is this: You'll ruin your dating life pretty quickly if you remain hopelessly devoted to your shallow requirements for a spouse. Look through your list [I know you have one]. And don't just look at the obvious problems like "good butt" [you should delete that, by the way]. Look also at the things that may seem deep but are actually just selfish and, dare I say, narrow-minded expectations. My shallow expectations kept me from seeing Ron the way I do now, which, when I think about it, makes me a little sad. Seriously, throw out your superficial little box and sit down and really pray to God about what your heart desires in a mate.

 QUESTIONS TO CONSIDER:

- What do you consider to be shallow?
- How shallow are you? Has one of your moments of shallowness ever messed up a relationship?
- Think about a moment in your dating history when another person's shallowness broke your heart. If you've had one of those experiences, how did it make you feel?
- How do you fight being shallow?

MISSIONARY DATING

[THE WORLD IS YOUR MISSION FIELD]

Many of us have done this: We meet someone who is hopelessly cute, hilarious, and brilliant, but unfortunately, this perfect specimen is not a Christian, which for most of us is a deal breaker. But we think, *If I can just show him the light of Christ, he will see clearly and become a Christian, and the rest will be history!* Hopefully, though, we all know the truth [though sadly I don't think we do because we continue to make the same mistake over and over again]: You will ruin your dating life if you continue to believe it's your mission from God to date unbelievers and win them over to Team Christianity. And to tell the truth, doing this is not all it's cracked up to be and is, quite frankly, more difficult than it looks!

The ministry in which I was involved in New York City, one that I so affectionately refer to as JFK [that's Jews for Kerri], is a prime example of missionary dating. Every time I visited NYC, I fell in love with a different Jewish man. I'd give him a Bible and say, "Read part 2: the *New* Testament. It gets better, kind of like *The Godfather: Part II*! You're only two holidays away from happily ever after."

But in all seriousness, I was a champion at dating Jewish men and doing whatever I could to bring them over to my team. It never worked. I had one serious Jewish boyfriend, Joshua Cohen, and it was like war of the religions between him and me. He wanted me to become Jewish, and I tried to convert him to Christianity. We eventually hit a standstill and broke up. When I finally got married, I received a gift from his mom, saying, "Thanks for not marrying my son!" I was so touched [and happy about the gift!].

No matter what you might think, doing the "dating outside your faith" thing is always a losing battle. Not to mention, it says in the Bible, "Do not be unequally yoked."* Technically you could be sinning by going against God's command. I believe the apostle Paul wrote that down so we wouldn't get stuck in a bad situation.

 QUESTIONS TO CONSIDER:

- Have you ever been guilty of missionary dating?
- What do you believe are the core problems of mixing dating and evangelism?
- What personality traits might a missionary dater have that would compel him or her to take this role?

SWM, 6'2", SEEKS PERFECTION

Whether we're willing to admit it or not, most of us expect perfection. Even if we think we're down to earth, we're not. Sure, we pretend to believe that no one's perfect, but we don't really believe it; we want our future spouse to be a spiritual

---

* See 2 Corinthians 6:14-15. We should note that while many Christians believe the "unequally yoked" verse is a reference to marriage, many biblical scholars disagree and say it's a reference to any grouping of people, not just husband and wife. Please study the different views for yourself prior to creating an opinion. Thank you!

Yoda, a hottie, an artist but also brilliant at taxes, and so on. But as Matthew and I (Kerri) have experienced, once you get married [which you will — don't be discouraged!], you will be, at times, sorely disappointed. And so will your spouse.

When I was in my midtwenties and really getting involved in church, several men who were old enough to have graduated from high school with my mom started having an interest in "walking/stalking" me to my car after church. On a couple of occasions, they looked my number up in the directory and called me to ask, "Would you like to get ice cream sometime?"

Ice cream?!?

I was like, *What is this, sixth grade?* I talked to my girlfriends about it, and they said the same thing happened to them until they turned about twenty-eight, and then those types of men deemed them too old. I even went on a date with this guy who turned out to be forty. He said he had just broken up with his girlfriend who was twenty [I know, I know] and he liked younger women because they were more "his speed." Oh, and he also wanted to have kids and was pretty sure that women over thirty wouldn't be able to bear his "seed." Okay, is that disgusting or what?

The more I look around, the more I see that a lot of men would rather date some swooning younger girl who might not bring as much life experience to the table than a thirtysomething woman. It's an easy way for them not to have to step up to the plate. It's possible I'm wrong about this theory [hardly], but look around and see for yourself. And this is but one perfect example of the curse of expecting perfection. Those men who pursue only twentysomething blondes are in for a bumpy road [and a few restraining orders] unless they open their minds *just* a little bit.

YES, MIRACLES DO HAPPEN, BUT THAT DOESN'T MEAN YOU SHOULDN'T FEEL THE STING OF REALITY!

[a few reality checks for Christian dating]

I (Matthew) will admit this sidebar is rather blunt. But all of us need a little tough love once in a while, right? Hey, I think it was Dr. Dobson who said those words; it wasn't me. So please take your issue up with him. But while you're thinking about the best way to speak your mind to the "Family" guy himself, why not first come face-to-face with some reality? Oh, and one more thing: *Most* of these reality checks are meant for men *and* women, regardless of my pronoun usage [yet some are gender specific; I think you'll be able to tell the difference].

- Just because both of you love Jesus doesn't mean you'll fit together like two puzzle pieces.

- Just because he loves Jesus doesn't mean he won't try to sleep with you [his moves will just be slower and guilt inducing].

- Just because she loves Jesus doesn't mean she will love you the way you are.

- Just because he loves Jesus doesn't mean he'll be attracted to obesity.

- Just because she loves Jesus doesn't mean she'll overlook your insulting her in public [and she shouldn't].

- Just because he loves Jesus doesn't mean he will want to pray with you every time you close your eyes and bow your head.

- Just because she loves Jesus doesn't mean she won't be, um, a [bleep] once in a while.

- Just because he loves Jesus doesn't mean he'll initiate the DTR.

- Just because she loves Jesus doesn't mean she'll understand your desire to hang with the guys once in a while.

- Just because he loves Jesus doesn't mean he won't decide to break up with you [for no real reason at all].

- Just because she loves Jesus doesn't mean she'll take you back after your spontaneous breakup.

- Just because both of you love Jesus doesn't mean you won't need a whole bunch of therapy to make your relationship work.

Now it's your turn. Try coming up with your own list! You might actually find it entertaining.

Both men and women have completely sabotaged their relationships due to unrealistic standards. As the list suggests, we hold numerous expectations [most of them subconscious] that will ultimately wound, if not totally ruin, our dating relationships. Believe me, once you're married, the uglier side of your loved one shows through, making dating look like a cinch. So if your expectations can't even get you through dating, you're in for big trouble in marriage. Think through that list again; it deals with deep-seated issues many of us don't even realize we have. And thinking through this now could save you a lot of time and hardship later.

QUESTIONS TO CONSIDER:

- Do you view yourself as perfect? Do you carry this need for perfection into your dating relationships?
- Is perfection ever a realistic expectation?
- What expectations in a member of the opposite sex could you let go of?
- How can the quality of humility help to eliminate the need for perfection?

Now that we're all good and humble, let's move on to the section for women!

THE LADIES' ROOM: STRONG ENOUGH FOR A MAN, BUT MADE FOR A WOMAN

I have found that a man will usually be as much a gentleman as a lady requires, and probably no more.

ELISABETH ELLIOT

Hey, ladies. What's up? It's me, Kerri, and now it's my turn to do the girl-to-girl, woman-to-woman, or whatever you want to call it section. But if you're a guy, you'd better be reading this stuff too. Matthew and I don't write this for our health; we write it so we can buy health insurance. Okay, that was a bad attempt at humor. I'm a professional; I should know better.

But seriously, in the section that follows I will attempt to tackle some of the topics you might not see in other dating books. Matthew and I wanted to write this book to go where no dating book has gone before. Guys, are you getting my *Star Trek* reference? I know, I'm cool. But sorry, I'm taken. We wanted to search for some truth regarding what's really going on out there in the Christian dating world. We all know we're sorely deprived of sermons on dating because most pastors won't touch the subject with a ten-foot pole. Sure, they'll talk about how sex is a sacred act you should save until marriage, but that's all I've ever heard from the pulpit. And the question of how far is too far is not the only struggle we Christians will encounter in our dating lives. I always longed to hear a sermon about being single and Christian in today's society. But I never did.

So while writing this book, Matthew and I interviewed singles to find out what topics they wanted us to write about and then compiled a list of things people can do to sabotage their dating lives. I can easily write about them because I've basically done them all. And if I haven't, I probably know someone who has. In this women's section, I've tried to use personal examples and, of course, random 1980s movie references whenever possible. I think God loves it when I bring up anything having to do with Corey Feldman or John Cusack.

The one challenge I faced when writing this part was the fact that, as you already know, I'm married. I blame my mother; she just wouldn't let up with the prayer circles and holy water. So, yes, there will be times when I'm giving advice to you single women and you're going to say, "Well, Kerri, that's easy for you to say! Why don't you go make out with your husband?" And it's fine if you want to say those things; I don't blame you. When I was single, I hated married people. They annoyed me because they could go have random romance or sex anytime they wanted to without feeling guilty.

But rather than hate me, think of it like this: Remember in the movie *A Christmas Carol* when Ebenezer Scrooge went to bed and was visited by Jacob Marley, his old business partner who was already dead and coming back to him from the other side? Well, in a way, you're Ebenezer and I'm Jacob Marley. I'm here to warn you of a few fatal mistakes you can avoid making before you enter "the other side," which I affectionately call wedded bliss. Of course, as you also already know, it took *a lot* of trial and error [mostly error] for me to finally get lucky, if you will, so I'm not just pulling this stuff out of thin air. You and I are, in some ways, in the same boat. So okay, here we go: how to ruin your dating life, girly-style.

WHAT YOU AS A GIRL CAN DO
TO RUIN YOUR DATING LIFE

USE SEXUALITY TO GET YOUR WAY
[you can choose Delilah as your role model — or Pamela Anderson!]

Okay, admit it, ladies: We've all read about the "bad girls" in the Bible and thought for one second that some of them seemed pretty cool, right? Think about it: Delilah had some serious power over Samson, and what woman wouldn't want that? But I promise that you will continue to ruin your dating life with any God-fearing man if you insist on playing the sexual card to win his attention.

Have I tried this and failed? Of course I have.

Let me take you back to my college years at the University of Michigan. Ah, it was the best of times and it was the worst of times. It was the 1990s, and more was still more in terms of hair, fashion, and cleavage. I wasn't blessed with a lot of natural cleavage, but I did what I could with what I was given. Victoria's Secret came in handy as well.

Back then, stores sold these amazing striped shirts that made objects in them appear larger than they actually were, if you get my drift. We actually had a name for them: the GS shirts. GS stood for Get Some! Yes, I'm admitting this in writing. Okay, stop judging me, you perfect little Christian angels. We would all rock these types of shirts out on the dance floor at the fraternity parties, knowing it would help us accomplish our goal of looking as hot as we were capable of at the ripe old age of eighteen. And it worked. Men would approach us with their tails wagging and tongues hanging out like salivating dogs. We loved the power, and we used it.

Unfortunately, I realize now that being sexy is an expected part of being a woman anywhere. We are bombarded with Hollywood and what the media tells us we need to do. It tells us we need to be HOT. There was an entire show called "Are You Hot Enough?" on Fox last season. We never once hear the word *hot* in the Bible unless someone is about to burn. Can you believe our culture has come up with the slang term *hot as hell*, and it's used to describe a good thing? We try to avoid temptations but nonetheless we women are obsessed with being enticing and wanted.

Christian women are not off the hook either. We, just like

the culture we live in, relish the attention of a man as we walk in the door and see his eyes widen and his tongue hang out a little. Have you seen some of the Christian awards shows lately? The gals aren't exactly in muu muus or turtleneck sweaters. What about some churches where you see the same outfits in the pews as you would in the nightclubs? We know how to "work what the good Lord gave us"! Does that mean we should? Does that mean cleavage is God's gift to us to share with the world? I see girls who are all of fourteen in miniskirts and tank tops with no bra singing "Shout to the Lord" as if there is nothing wrong with their attire at all. Why would they think there is if no one tells them any differently? Or what about the moms and daughters at church functions who both look like they're dressing for a Britney Spears look-alike contest?

Okay, so I'm being a little dramatic, but it is obviously a hugely debatable topic, and I think every one of us knows when we've taken it too far. I mean, we can play dumb and say we don't mean to be overly provocative, but take a good look in the mirror and ask yourself if you're overstepping the line. I know we want to be hip, and I'm not expecting us to stop keeping up with the trends. But maybe we can just be a bit more careful when we dress to be hot and in fashion.

I remember I bought the Victoria's Secret water bra when it was introduced. I still have it. I love that thing. I'm like a warrior princess in it. I'm like She-Ra Princess of Power. "I have the power!" because it makes my bra size increase by about two cups. It's awesome and fun. I used to pair that bra up with major cleavage shirts, and it just wasn't a nice thing to do to my dates. Talk about false advertising!

Don't you girls have a "date outfit"? You have that one outfit you know makes heads turn, and you usually like to rock that out on a first date, right? When I was going on my first date with Ron, I put on my "date shirt"/water bra combo. Would you believe I actually got convicted from the Lord? I'm not kidding. I felt like God was saying, "You know this guy is Christian. How do you want him to see you? For the godly woman you are or as a piece of meat?" I changed clothes. That was a big milestone for me. I showed up with my regular cute sweater and took a chance he would like me without all the "enhancements." We had a great time, and obviously it worked. I'm not saying I don't still rock the water bra on occasion, but I'm not pairing it with shirts cut down to my navel like my girl J.Lo.

I heard this awesome quote by an anonymous writer: "It takes an entire crew of makeup artists, hair stylists, and photo retouchers to make one supermodel look the way a man in love sees his wife every day." The times Ron tells me I look the most beautiful aren't when I'm rocking out the sequins and hairspray. They're usually when I'm rolling out of bed with my flannel pajamas on and I'm just plain old me. That's who he married, and he loves me unconditionally, with or without my water bra.

SEXY OR SLUTTY?

[a thought or two from Matthew]

I have met so many women who obsess over how they look. One of my friends refuses to go outside her house without spending a good ninety minutes on her appearance. That's not only ridiculous, but it's self-centered and unnecessary. Kerri's right: Culture has turned us into maniacs regarding outside appearances. But the crazy thing is that *most guys prefer girls who are natural and comfortable in their own skin.* Guys don't always do the best job of revealing that preference — mostly because we're a little self-consumed too — but it's true; guys are more attracted to natural beauty than made-up beauty. Sure, guys like it when girls show some pride and care in the way they look, but our idea of beauty and theirs seem to be very different a lot of the time. *Guys think confidence is sexy.* Hopefully that revelation will help you avoid fretting when you're standing in front of the mirror attempting to get ready. And when it comes to how you dress, *be yourself.*

TRAVEL IN HERDS

[the surefire way to freak a guy out]

We all know that women are not cattle [though we sometimes feel like cows], so there is no reason you have to travel with sixteen of your closest friends to every occasion. You will ruin your dating life if you continue to travel in herds.

My girlfriends and I used to have a nightly ritual in college. I lived in the Alpha Phi sorority with about sixty of my closest friends. Hey, we were sisters! We did everything together. On those cold winter nights, we could cram about eighteen of us into one car if we tried. We looked like a clown car from the circus.

We'd finish watching *Melrose Place* at nine and then go upstairs to primp for an hour or so. At ten we'd double-check each other's makeup and attire and head out the door, all sixty of us. We'd go to a fraternity party and find some part of the room to plop down on couches and stare at every guy as he walked by. My friend Julie and I were like the judges from *American Idol*. Well, we were more like the judges from *The Muppets*. We'd give every guy the once over with our arms crossed, looking him up and down. And then we wondered why no one ever approached us.

We'd then take matters into our own hands, grab about nineteen sisters, and hit the dance floor. We'd form a huge circle and wait for songs like "Brown Eyed Girl." Then we'd prance around like witches around a caldron, circling each other and singing. We thought we had it made but again wondered why no men approached us. Well, almost no men. Sometimes one brave, usually intoxicated soul would try to shuffle up to our inner sanctum, and it was a brutal sight to see him completely ignored and humiliated in front of all his laughing friends. We'd do this until about one in the morning and then pile back into our car, stopping for pizza and giggling all the way back to our home. Then we'd stay up all night talking about what a lame party it was because none of the guys, except the scary ones, gave us any attention. We just thought the rest of them were cowards.

What's wrong with this picture? Absolutely nothing at the

time. But after a while, we all discovered that the man we'd eventually marry would want to be with *us*, not all our girlfriends, so stepping out alone would be necessary.

I remember one time I tried to make it on my own. My married friends invited me to their Christmas party, and I knew there would at least be really good food amid lots of married people with babies. I showed up all by myself. This was a huge step for me. I arrived and focused my sights on this cute guy in a Santa scarf. He looked fun and festive and kind of dorky. I grabbed the first baby I saw because I thought it would make me look approachable and maternal. Also, our outfits matched a little. He came over and we engaged in small talk for about five lovely minutes. I could tell he was into me because he kept smiling at the cute baby and me. Then he informed me I was holding HIS BABY! Strike one for the home team. I binged out on a cheese log for the rest of the night, so it wasn't a total loss.

Girls, I realize now that we make ourselves as approachable as an ice queen when a guy feels like he has to get through eighteen other ladies to even speak to us. Why do we make it so hard for him? If a guy finds you attractive at a social event, he shouldn't have to fight military style through your friends/ bodyguards to introduce himself, should he? Think of the way your body language is at parties. Do you and your friends huddle up like the Green Bay Packers around the punch bowl? Do you sit on a couch staring at everyone who walks by and make dumb comments? Even if you don't make comments about them, guys assume you're judging them just by the way you're acting. The next time you're out, take a look around and see if I'm right.

I'm not saying there is an exact science to making yourself

seem friendly if you're out with your girls. But if you're at an event and you'd like to meet someone new, here are some things to ponder: Consider bringing only one friend along instead of your entire sorority. Be open to meeting new people. Guys aren't exactly the best with opening lines, so go easy on them. And don't be afraid to greet the cute guy across the room yourself. He'll love that you were confident enough to take a step in his direction!

KERRI'S TOP TEN

[things your mother was right about concerning men and dating]

1. Guys would rather call you first.
2. A little lipstick is never a bad idea.
3. Nice girls finish first! Be a nice girl.
4. Don't talk with your mouth full, and mind your manners. Men will appreciate it.
5. No man will ever love you like your father does. He thinks you're a princess.
6. Good dancers and suave men are overrated. Marry a nice boy. He'll treat you the way you deserve to be treated.
7. Trust in the Lord and lean not on your own understanding. He has someone special picked out just for you.
8. Marry for love, not money.
9. The water bra is false advertising. You want a man to love you for what's above your neck.
10. Act like a lady and you will be treated like one.

PLAN YOUR WEDDING ON THE FIRST DATE
[nothing makes a man run faster]

It's true that every woman dreams about her wedding day from childbirth. But you *will* ruin your dating life if you think you should get a marriage proposal on date two. Or three. Or even twenty. We've already discussed how effective neediness is, so you can imagine how the problems multiply when you begin planning your wedding to a man you just met. Worse still [if that's possible] is the old "we're practically married" trick. Women *love* the idea of having a man as theirs and will manipulate every word to make all appearances look that way. We go goo goo ga ga over every milestone [your two-weeks-since-we-first-kissed anniversary is *not* reason to celebrate]. Stuff like that scares guys off. Don't show up at his office or in front of all his friends on your two-month anniversary with a potted plant or a picture of the two of you. This is not okay behavior and makes you look entirely too codependent.

The thing is, we all do it. Call it what you want: jumping the gun, rushing the relationship, whatever. We women are such control freaks. We can't wait five minutes for a relationship to develop naturally. We're too busy trying to create the perfect love affair before it even begins.

Here are some ways to prevent falling into this dangerous pothole:

1. Turn off Lifetime and any movie having to do with overnight romances. That includes anything starring Julia Roberts, Meg Ryan, or Reese Witherspoon. Keep in

mind that in real life, each of them has had her own ups and downs when it comes to relationships. I rest my case.

2. Stop reading magazines that highlight the "Top 20 Ways to Get a Man." Next month you'll be reading the "Top 20 Ways to Keep Your Man" or the "Top 20 Ways to Steal a Man." These pieces are written mostly by gay men or single women in NYC. Don't believe the hype.

3. Don't take quizzes to find out what your man is thinking. Also, don't even think about trying to make him take a quiz. He will run and not come back, I promise. Try something crazy instead: If you want to know what he's thinking and you're supposedly in an honest and open dialogue, ask him. I know it's like pulling teeth to get men to open up, but it's worth a shot. Disclaimer here: Asking doesn't mean nagging. But if there is a certain subject you're really curious about, such as, "Do you see me as a potential long-term girl-friend?" you have every right to ask.

4. On a first date, try not to bring your wish list of the perfect mate and check it off at the table. Things change. People change. And just because he doesn't meet your weight requirement doesn't give you the right to talk to him about joining a gym with you. In fact, on the first few dates, it's best not to try to plan too many future activities together. Some of you are thinking right now, *Thanks, Captain Obvious; I know.* But you'd be surprised how many of us women can become *terrifying* when we're desperate.

5. Don't invite him to meet your parents yet. Wait until the meeting seems excruciatingly overdue. And then wait another two weeks.

6. Live in the moment. This isn't a movie. You have more than 122 minutes to fall in love. Enjoy the experience.

Dating is so insecure. My last relationship, I was always there for her and she dumped me. I told her about it. I said, "Remember when your grandma died? I was there. Remember when you flunked out of school? I was there. Remember when you lost your job? I was there!" She said, "I know — you're bad luck."

TOM ARNOLD

WHEN THINGS ARE GOING WELL, ENTERTAIN [THE EASY WAY] FOR THAT SPECIAL SOMEONE

If you want to do something special for your loved one and you're short on the Martha Stewart gene, don't worry. Here are a few tricks that are surefire winners anyone can do:

1. Instead of making some elaborate meal from scratch, go to your local market, like Whole Foods Market or Bristol Farms, and order from the premade deli section. Ask the man at the counter to make you an assortment of great finger foods like cheeses, meats, olives, dips, and breads. You can take it home and

display it however you'd like on one of your plates, and you'll have a smorgasbord of delights. Ask him to go light on garlicky treats, just in case.

2. Invite your SO over for a night of fun and chocolate. Serve a buffet of decadence. At www.hersheys.com you can even order a big chocolate bar, and they will put a name or personal message on the wrapper. Be like two little kids: Skip dinner and go right for the good stuff. Add a little red wine for effect.

3. Learn how to boil rice and chop vegetables. Add them to any of those frozen entrees in a bag and it will look like a homemade specialty.

4. Make cooking a learning experience for both of you. Together you can pick out a recipe for a simple meal you want to prepare and make a date of it. My friend learned to cook that way with her fiancé, and now they continue the tradition of making a new recipe once a week. You can even invite friends over to cook with you and trade ideas. It's affordable and a great way to get to know someone — especially to see if he knows how to follow directions!

DATE ONLY THE BAD BOYS
[and let the savior complex take the reins]

Girls, girls, girls! Remember that song "Bad Boys"? No, it's not sexy. It's the theme song from the show *COPS*! Does that tell us something? Bad boys usually stay bad. It's not up to us to save them. Where in the Bible does it tell us we're supposed to do Jesus' job? I know this lesson all too well. I've had the "Kerri Poppins" complex for years.

THE LADIES' ROOM: STRONG ENOUGH FOR A MAN, BUT MADE FOR A WOMAN

You remember the movie *Mary Poppins*? With just a "spoonful of sugar" she brought joy and laughter to an entire family that was down in the dumps. Mr. Grouchy George Banks was a bad boy of sorts, and she even made him sing a happy song and dance a little jig. Since I was a little girl, I've taken on the "Kerri Poppins" persona and believed that each manic-depressive, chain-smoking rebel without a clue in a leather jacket just needed a little "sugar from Kerri" and we'd be singing in no time. I know you sense the theme here — I watch too many movies. But think about it: Hollywood and society constantly glorify the "good girl tames bad boy" story line. They just don't tell you that most of the couples the media loves to cover end in divorce. I mean, who wouldn't want some version of Johnny Depp tattooing her name on his arm? Or being the woman who tamed the "wild man"?

YOUR QUESTION, MY OPINION

QUESTION:

Hello, dating book,

I consider myself a good catch. I have a good job and good friends with whom I spend my time on weekends. I love my family and take care of my two dogs like they are my kids. I love God and want to get married. I may not be Mr. Supermodel, but I'm not bad-looking. What's wrong with me? Why can't I get a date? I ask girls out, but I'm always looked at as "Mr. Nice Guy" or "the friend." Do I need to be more of a bad boy because those guys get chicks? Do I need an extreme image makeover or what? Help!

David, 30

ANSWER:
Dave!

Please don't believe the hype! *Girls* want bad boys. *Women* want nice men! I promise, Dave, it's going to be okay. But stop looking for immature little girls who can't handle a real man. You don't need an image makeover unless you have some glaring problem. Do you have any female friends who can be brutally honest with you about your approach with women? They are the best resources, and they can take you shopping if they have to. Fashion therapy is never a bad idea. Showering regularly helps too. Women find the smell of soap on a man very hot.

Kerri

We women can't resist a challenge. Even when I was first starting to have feelings for Ron, he said, "I just don't want a girlfriend right now. I'm too busy with my career." Well, the voice inside my head was saying, "Ding, ding, ding... let the games begin! Now I must have him!" It's like we're in some poker match and we want to win "the man who doesn't want to be tamed" as our trophy. They should call it "trophy boyfriend" instead of "trophy wife." Admit it, ladies: We play the same games the guys do, and, in my opinion, we're much craftier. But it's not what God wants us to do. It's not a good idea for us to get involved with yet another bad boy just so our egos can inflate. These types of guys will most likely hurt us in the end. Now, I bet you want me to define *bad boy*. I'll give it my best shot:

- **This guy doesn't want a girlfriend [i.e., commitment].** Though you pretend to, you don't listen to him.

You think you're charming and wonderful and will absolutely change his mind. Once he sees how magical spending time with you is, he'll come around and become a committed, faithful boyfriend and husband-to-be in no time. Let me tell you something about this type of guy: He doesn't want a girlfriend for a reason. He wants to see several women and keep his options open. If you force him into a commitment with guilt and manipulation, he will very likely cheat on you or just break your heart. Or sometimes this type of guy has deep-seated emotional issues he hasn't dealt with yet. He is not capable of committing to one woman and is kind enough to warn you. Believe him!

- **This guy has destructive habits you can't stand.**

    a. He chain-smokes.
    b. He does drugs of any kind.
    c. *Party* is the primary verb in his vocabulary.

Let me address this type of guy. We've all dated him. Mine wore cool leather jackets and had long hair. He was quiet and brooding and told me I was his angel. I didn't know he'd end up being my devil! Okay, maybe it didn't go that far. But we were together for a long time, and he kept promising me he was going to stop smoking, drinking, and doing all the other things I kept begging him to cut out. He gave it an honest effort [at least I think he did]. But you know what happened? He just ended up resenting me for trying to change him,

and he continued to smoke and party behind my back.
It got really messy and I cried a lot. I stayed with him
because his personality was enticing. He was dramatic,
and when I'd threaten to leave, he'd cry and write me a
poem about how I was his only hope.

We were in a bad cycle and neither of us saw it. I
just wanted to be important to someone, and this guy
made me feel like his lifeline. I see now how unhealthy
that was. A lot of you are in relationships exactly like
this one right now, and you don't have the strength to
leave because you're pulled in too tight. Maybe your
boyfriend has gone way over the edge and threatened
to hurt himself if you leave. This is not okay, and if
this is happening, I strongly suggest you seek some
wise counsel immediately. There is always help if you're
willing to get it.

- **He doesn't respect authority or the need for
  accountability.** One time I was dating a guy named
  Max. I was starting to get involved with my church,
  and in doing so I met a wonderful lady named
  Maritza. She quickly became a mentor and counselor
  to me in many ways. I was so excited to meet a godly
  woman I could go to for prayer and advice. When I
  told Max about her at church and wanted to introduce
  him to her, he walked out the door. He wouldn't even
  meet her. I was totally embarrassed and had to make
  up some lame excuse for his abrupt departure. If you're
  dating a guy who doesn't want you seeking godly counsel, you should not be dating him. End of story.

At the same time, you need to be involved with someone who desires God's wisdom in all areas of his life as well. Whether he finds it through a men's Bible study or by meeting one-on-one with an older mentor, this is essential.

Finally, though the two of you need not broadcast the details of all your intimate late-night talks, you do need accountability in your dating because it's hard to keep on the straight and narrow, especially in the purity department.

BE HIGH MAINTENANCE
[a status for cars, not girls]

For ages men have accused us, the fairer sex, of being the ever-popular high maintenance. Once in a while it's funny, but if you find that men call you high maintenance all the time, you might wonder if you're *trying* to be high maintenance. I know I've done it many times. I have a very Southern mother who raised me to believe that we ladies don't need to do a lot of heavy lifting or manual labor in life, if you catch my drift. My father caters to her every need. She hasn't walked from a parked car to a restaurant door since the 1970s. It's all in the way she conducts herself. For my mother, it works. For the rest of us, it usually flops.

I remember when I failed the eHarmony quiz because they had no matches for me. That thing asked 1,209,840 questions, and obviously I must have crashed the system with my responses. They were supposed to dig into my inner mind and then find my perfect soul mate. They offered this grand service for only forty bucks! What a deal! So I did it. And they didn't have any matches for me. I think they even inferred that I was expecting too much out of a man [i.e., high maintenance]. *What?* I thought. *That's just another way of saying I'm Southern!* I was insulted. Why couldn't they find me a nice man like my dad? He puts up with my mother and all her little wants and needs. It's how I was raised. It's not my fault!

The funny thing is that most of us women classify ourselves as really laid back. It wasn't until I was married that I realized what a total control freak I am. Ladies, we want men to pursue us. We want our boyfriends and husbands to take good care of us. But we don't want to drive them out the door screaming to an early grave. Being high maintenance will ruin your dating life!

Okay, you say, but what is the difference between being high maintenance and having high standards? Consider this question: On a date, do you expect the man to

a. pay for everything all the time?
b. meet you at the door with flowers all the time?
c. plan romantic outings and picnics all the time?
d. tell you that you are beautiful and angelic all the time?
e. all of the above ALL THE TIME?

I think you would need to be blonder than me *not* to get this picture. Even so, some of you *don't* get the picture; you think this list is perfectly acceptable. If so, you are HIGH MAINTENANCE.

We women have the difficult job of balancing strength and high expectations without being totally demanding. It's not easy to know exactly where to draw the line. And it's not like we have many emotionally healthy relationship models out there with today's high divorce rate.

The other struggle we face in this conundrum is the recent confusion of gender roles. Women, bless our hearts, have become so obsessed with being capable that men are sometimes not even sure where they fit into our plan. I've talked to men who say, "If I open a car door for a woman, she thinks I'm sending the message that she can't do it herself." And then there are those of us who would prefer that a gentleman always open a door for us because that is how we were brought up. Who's right? It depends on who you are and also who you are dating. It's important to look at the man you're spending time with and determine if he treats you in a way you're comfortable with. If receiving flowers is a deal breaker for you, then you have to be honest about that. Don't expect men to guess at what you want. Also be realistic. Don't be overly demanding. That takes all the fun out of anything romantic. Try to be more subtle. If you pass a flower shop, pointing out that you happen to love pink roses is okay. Sending your boyfriend a list of local florists who already have your preferences in the computer is not okay. And if a guy tries to do something nice for you but it's not up to your standards, that is no reason to negate his gesture. It really is the thought behind it that counts. It's a good idea to review your past dating experiences and consider whether your expectations were ever a little over the top.

Being high maintenance is ultimately just a glossier version of selfishness, which makes it a heart issue that each of us has to look into on our own. Ask God to show you where you have been selfish in your relationships and to give you a loving and serving heart. It's what marriage is all about, and it's better to learn these lessons now. It may seem cute and charming to be that "diva with the feva," but trust me, that act wears really thin when you get down to being in a long-term relationship in which giving is a two-way street.

BELIEVE A GUY SHOULD FIND YOU PERFECT *EXACTLY* AS YOU ARE RIGHT NOW
[and watch him fail miserably and resent you for it]

On the other side of the high-maintenance coin is our belief that our man may need to change, but we are perfect just as we are. We believe we are in the right 99.9 percent of the time. We adhere to the words of the great songwriters of our time: "Don't go changing; it won't please me!" Insist that you are near perfect, and you will ruin your dating life.

We have to accept a cold, hard reality. Sometimes we are the ones who need to change. I think this is one of the most difficult truths I've ever had to deal with. My husband wanted to buy me a sign that said, "I don't play well with others." I was so very, very set in my ways by the time we got together that he barely stood a chance. Once in a while, he would graciously point out something about me that needed some restructuring, and I would bite his head off, exclaiming, "You're trying to change me!" Guess what? He was. And that's okay. When poor Ron came along and noticed some of my little habits, he thought bringing them to my attention might not be a bad thing. He was right, but he was also so very wrong, poor guy.

For instance, I've never been one to tightly screw the tops

on jars or pens. It never bothered me that one out of four times something spilled or that a lot of my furniture displayed small pen marks. I didn't notice. Ron did. He also noticed that I some times left the lights on — and even the stove on one occasion. He would try to gently remind me that these behaviors weren't always the best plan of action. Instead of kindly accepting his reminders, I'd blurt out, "I'm thirty! I can do it myself! I'm a big girl and I've been doing this alone for a long time, so back it up, buddy!" I sounded like a ranting six-year-old. One time he was about to remind me that I hadn't screwed the top on tightly to a huge jar of powdered Tang. He saw the look on my face as I was about to open it and decided to remain quiet. In three seconds flat there was bright orange Tang all over my new outfit and the entire kitchen floor. I could see that Ron was about to burst out laughing, and secretly so was I. But that would admit to his being right and my being wrong. I just shot him a "Don't you even say it" look, turned around in my Tang-stained blouse, and started cleaning. Another one of Ron's favorite moments was when I was making brownies for him and they weren't cooking. I decided to stick them back in the oven on broil so they'd cook faster. Ron thought this was a bad idea, and once again I rebuked him. I said, "I've been doing this brownie thing for years, kiddo, and I haven't seen your Betty Crocker cookbooks, so just let me do my thing."

I stepped out of the kitchen, and five minutes later all I could smell was smoke permeating my entire apartment. I raced into the kitchen, and inside the oven I could see flames. I opened the door to rescue the burning brownies only to discover that my entire baking dish had broken into three pieces. I saw Ron peek around the corner, and this time he didn't say a word. He just snapped his camera, creating what he later affectionately referred to as evidence. He also had the pleasure of e-mailing the picture to all of his friends and our families. I've never cooked for him since, so I guess it worked out better in the long run.

These are just some small, fun examples of Ron's trying to help or change me. But seriously, the issue wasn't my lack of baking skills or my forgetfulness with the lids. It was the fact that I was so completely pigheaded that I wouldn't allow him to step in and help me.

Girls, if we're so perfect — and that's the message we're putting out to our boyfriends and potential husbands — then what do we need them for? That's really what we're saying. Men want to feel like we need them. If we're honest with ourselves, we know we do need them at the most important times in our lives, not just when the check comes after dinner or when we have heavy luggage that needs to be carried. God created marriage between two people as a partnership, and that requires us ladies to let a guy in to be that partner. But this is very difficult for us, and I believe there are several reasons that contribute to that:

1. **Society tells us we don't need a man.** And, worse, society tells us we don't even need God. Look at the magazine ads expressing to women, "You can have it all! All by yourself!" Yay! Well, if you wanted to be all by yourself, I doubt you'd be reading this book. So let's assume you don't agree with this message. Don't listen to the hype.

2. **We're afraid of letting someone into our lives because we might get hurt.** I know we've all been there before. We let a guy in too fast and get comfortable having him around, and the next thing we know he bolts out the door, never to return. I can't promise that won't happen again, because letting someone get close to you is always going to be a risk. But here is one way to look at it: If you're dating someone and you enjoy his company and respect him as a person, just listen to what he has to say. Treat him with respect and think, *If this were a parent or a good friend trying to give me the same advice, how would I respond?* Maybe he's not the one you'll marry, but it can't hurt to make some positive changes now, can it?

3. **We're afraid to take a look at ourselves because we might not like what we see.** Ladies, our insecurities may be buried deeper than we think, but it doesn't help us to pretend they aren't there. If you really care about being the best you can be in a relationship and hopefully a marriage someday, isn't it about time you looked at some of the things about yourself that might be holding you back? So what if there are things you need to change? Who cares? You're not perfect! No one is even close. So just realize that God still made you to be an amazing, caring woman. We're all a work in progress. It definitely takes a humble heart to accept the fact that God is refining you. It's like in the Bible where God says he's refining us like precious gold and silver. If you think of change in the way God describes,

it's easier to swallow. Praying to God to help you see yourself the way he sees you is a great step in this process.

On the opposite side of this spectrum, I will readily admit there are limits to changing yourself as a response to the opposite sex. You have to determine if the changes your loved one wants you to make are reasonable and healthy. Are you changing *for* him or *because* of his wise insight? There is a *big* difference.

For instance, if he frequently complains about the way you dress or style your hair, maybe this isn't the right guy for you. [And if he's that into fashion, you might be a little scared in the first place.] I've always chosen to date men who aren't prettier than I am, if you get my drift. I don't need the competition. Or if he makes a habit of embarrassing or correcting you in public, this is not the right guy for you. The point is, there are some things that aren't constructive criticism but rather nitpicking, which can turn into destructive patterns very quickly.

On the other hand, if your SO offers you the kind of insight that improves you as a human being, stick with him and take his advice.

Now, I'm not trying to make an Oprah episode about this, and you will certainly *not* find a "What's wrong with you?" quiz in this entire book. This is a personal journey between you and God. The thing I want to communicate is that men are not the enemy. If there's a man in your life and you know he cares about you and has your best interests in mind, then treat him with the respect he deserves and regard his opinion. It's going to save you time and anger in the long run. And if you're open to his contribution, just think: He might, in return, allow you to raid his closet! Change is good!

MARRY IMMEDIATELY FOLLOWING PUBERTY
[good for Mary and Joseph, killer for you — unless you live in Uganda]

You want to ruin your dating life? Make sure you get married right after puberty before you know what you really want.

I can cite you example after example of girls who specifically went to college to get their MRS degree. And you very well may be one of those girls. It's an epidemic and it needs to stop. Ladies, if you *need* to get married and are obsessed with being hitched by nineteen, you have a problem. This is a good idea about .01 percent of the time.

I know some of you found the love of your life at sixteen. My best friend in high school, Susie, had a mad crush on this boy named Ryan ever since she saw him skateboard around town in eighth grade. In eleventh grade Ryan didn't have a date for homecoming, so I set him up with Mia, my other friend. Susie got jealous. He dumped Mia and dated Susie and now they're married. End of story. Yes, it happens. But *not* very often. And, by the way, they waited until they were in their early twenties to get married. They didn't run off to the chapel after high school graduation.

Ron has this theory that every little girl has been planning her wedding since the age of zygote. He says we weren't having tea parties as little girls but rather planning our wedding seating chart. Maybe he's right. I always dreamed about the special day when I'd waltz down the aisle in some stunning white dress to the prince waiting for me at the altar and we'd say some vows and live happily every after. Unfortunately, I had to kiss a lot of toads before I met him, but he was worth waiting for [sorry for the cliché]. But that's another book entirely.

We may want to get married, but we have to be willing to wait on God's best for us. And that *might* mean we have some growing up to do in the meantime. Of course, it's true when they say that no one is fully prepared for marriage. God isn't keeping you from marriage until you're ready; he's not mad at you; he doesn't think you're uglier than everyone else or that your personality just isn't conducive to marriage. Rather, he has his plans and intends on sticking to them. Ask most married Christian women and they'll tell you they are *so* glad they waited until the timing was right.

Marriage is never easy for anyone, and you may be selling yourself short if you rush into this lifelong situation before it's the right time. And this doesn't apply only to adolescent marriages; it applies to all of us whether we are eighteen, twenty, twenty-five, twenty-seven, thirty-five, or forty-five. However old you are, God hasn't forgotten about you. Just don't rush him.

I'm sure you know that Paul was right when he said his focus was solely on God when he was single. That's a blessing, he said. Many married Christian women will tell you that their relationship with God went through several changes after they were married; namely, they didn't spend as much time with him because they were busy being a wife. This, too, is part of God's plan. But during your single years, as annoying and *hard* as it can be, embrace your relationship with God. It is truly a special one-on-one time that many married women mourn the loss of. I know, you're *so* annoyed with me right now. But I speak the truth!

PRETEND TO BE SOMEONE YOU'RE NOT
[the perfect way to marry the wrong guy]

Ladies, if you think pretending to be the perfect woman in the perfect package is going to help your dating life, you're mistaken! Pretending to be someone you're not is a great way to ruin your dating life. I've done it way too many times. It never works because you can't pretend forever.

My mother is a domestic goddess. She throws fabulous dinner parties and is always the hostess with the mostest. She never misses a beat. Of course, I inherited absolutely none of these traits. I couldn't sew a button on if you paid me a hundred bucks. I don't cook much, and when I do, it's not pretty. But when I was single, I was nonetheless convinced that all men wanted to marry a woman like my mom. I wanted all the guys I dated to be enamored by my [imaginary] culinary skills so they would know I was wife material. It didn't stop there. When I dated guys who liked the outdoors, I would pretend to be "Ms. Tree Hugger." If a guy were an intellectual, I'd quote from my best poetry repertoire, like Shel Silverstein and Dr. Seuss.

When I started dating this guy Randy, a cutie from South

Carolina, he often suggestively mentioned how he missed his mom's Southern home cooking. Of course, I knew all about Southern cooking; I just didn't know how to do it. But I played it up like I was some super home-cooking chef. After a while, I couldn't put it off any longer. I had to show him my super chef skills because he was begging me to cook for him, so I invited him over for dinner one night. I was so excited and freaked out at the same time.

At about two o'clock, I realized I had no idea what I was doing. Yes, I had ten cookbooks in my kitchen, but the dust on them was so thick you could barely get them open. I picked out recipes that seemed easy, but I was not making any progress at all. So I called my neighbor Tim, who actually knows how to cook. I said, "Tim! This is Kerri! You have to help me. Randy is coming over at six thirty, and I told him I'd make him my special recipe for jambalaya and all the fixins. By the way, what are fixins, anyway? I'm dead! Can you please help? He thinks I know how to cook!" Tim replied, "Why on earth would he think that, Kerri?" "Because I told him I could, of course! Duh! Now get over here pleeeeeeeeease!" I shouted in desperation.

So Tim came to my rescue. He helped me cook a bag of jambalaya stuff from Trader Joe's. My whole kitchen started to smell like home cooking. The aroma of seafood and spices actually smelled like jambalaya! I was elated. This was going to work. I then took some spice jars out of my cabinet and laid them out on the counter as if they had been used to create my masterpiece. Then I threw the bag away — in a garbage can far from the kitchen.

At four forty-five I got cocky. I endeavored to actually

cook something I had seen my mom make a million times: her famous Broccoli Cheese Corn Bread. It seemed really easy. I could follow directions after all, couldn't I? All I needed was milk, cheese, broccoli, and corn bread mix from a box. It would be a snap. I did pretty well until midway through the recipe when I realized that the corn bread mix I had bought was not plain corn bread but blueberry corn bread. I didn't have time to waste, so I just kept cooking and picked out a few blueberries from the batter. I didn't think it would matter. Why not enjoy Broccoli Cheese Blueberry Corn Bread? That could be a new twist, right? He'd love it.

I set the table with the plates my mom gave me that I almost never used. I lit the candles and used the "good napkins," and everything looked perfect. I found an apron in the bottom kitchen drawer that belonged to my roommate and actually put it on. When Randy arrived, I had applied my makeup perfectly so I could give the impression that even after a hard day of working in the kitchen, I would always look absolutely stunning, eyelashes curled and everything. My hair was pulled back with that tussled sexy look. I had applied my favorite perfume so I would smell like antique rose instead of corn bread. [I had read in *Cosmo* that men are attracted to that particular scent for whatever reason.] I was ready to rock and roll.

When Randy arrived, I could tell he was impressed. I served him first, and we sat down to enjoy the fruits of my labor. He raved about the jambalaya, saying it was absolutely the best he had ever had. I said coyly, "Oh, it's just something I threw together. No big deal."

About a minute later, we bit into my concoction of Broccoli

Cheese Blueberry Corn Bread. We almost choked, but neither of us said anything. The stuff was so disgusting I wouldn't even feed it to the dog. It was just gross. Not only was it undercooked, but the blueberries had mixed in with the melted cheese and broccoli florets, creating a big purple and green mess. My gut instinct was to burst out laughing, but I didn't know this guy very well, and I wasn't sure he would think it was funny. I could tell he didn't know how to handle the situation. It was awkward, to say the least. I tried to ignore his attempts to place his corn bread deep inside his napkin in his lap. Every time I turned my head, I saw him try to spit it out. It was a nightmare. I was cracking up inside, but I didn't let him see that side of me. This was years ago, and I didn't think being the "funny girl" would be a turn-on. I was trying to be the demure domestic girl back then.

Our meal ended politely, and overall I could tell he was pleased with my efforts. I was relieved that the rest of the meal probably made him forget about my corn bread experiment. As I walked him to the door, he said, "Kerri, this was just great. When can I come back for another tasting?" And he was totally serious. I had convinced this guy that cooking was such a hobby of mine that it would be no big deal to feed him on a regular basis. I had dug my own hole, and I didn't see a way out. Luckily our relationship fizzled shortly thereafter and I didn't have to continue the cooking charade for much longer.

You'd think that would have taught me a lesson, wouldn't you? But no. I had a boyfriend who was a dog lover, so I pretended to like dogs. [I hate dogs. Stop judging me; I just do. I think animals are a waste of space.] I had to let his mangy, hair-ridden, flea-covered dogs lick me and fart all over me. It was beyond torture, and every time it happened, my boyfriend would say, "Oh, he must like you. He's so comfortable around you!" Thank God that I married a Korean and that his people actually eat this type of animal. [I said STOP judging me! I can't help what my people do! I'm Asian now! I might be kidding, but even so, I have no dogs.]

Needless to say, I needed to break my pattern of faking it. I was sabotaging any possibility of a real relationship because in the process of trying to impress a man, I was losing the real me. At some point in our lives, almost all of us women do this. Of course we all play our "A game" at the beginning of a relationship, but our best behaviors *will* fade away to reveal our true selves. What will you do then? Your true self is just as lovable as your perfect persona, so why reject her for the sake of a guy you're not compatible with anyway?

Some of you know exactly what I'm talking about because you've been that girl too. I don't know why we can't just speak up for ourselves if there's something we don't want to do. I have a theory: This comes from women being such people pleasers that we don't want to let anyone down. We want everyone to be happy, and if that means compromising ourselves, well, we just do it. This is not okay. This is not what God means when he tells us to be unselfish. It's fake and disingenuous. If you start off a relationship being someone you're not, it's only going to get you into trouble. So what if you don't like to hike and you've never seen the inside of a gym?

I ended up with Ron, who is a master at the fine art of sleeping and eating. When we vacation, we might as well be with the senior citizens because all we do is sleep in, eat ourselves silly, take a nap, and then plan where we're going out to dinner. It's a beautiful thing. He doesn't golf. He doesn't play tennis. We just sit there and do nothing. It's a match made in heaven.

WATCH TOO MANY CHICK FLICKS

[it will drive you to do very foolish things]

> If I'm such a legend, why am I so lonely?
>
> JUDY GARLAND

I know I've said this a million times already, but I've always tried to live like I'm in a Turner Classic Movie. Sadly, my romances usually ended up more like a bad reality TV show. I think one of the most dangerous things we women can do is watch too many chick flicks and try to emulate those relationships ourselves.

From *Pretty Woman* to *Bridget Jones's Diary*, the world is full of messages that aren't even close to the way true love works. Take Julia Roberts in *Pretty Woman*. It goes like this: Girl becomes prostitute. Prostitute meets rich man who is good-looking. He pays her money. They have sex but don't kiss. She eats strawberries. He hires her. She goes shopping with his money. He falls for her in new clothes and dresses her up in diamonds. He tells her he loves her and wants to rescue her/ marry her, and they kiss. Roll the credits.

Or consider Bridget Jones: Girl gets job in office and starts the sexual Olympics with her hot and cocky boss, played by Hugh Grant. She acts like a total hussy, and they kiss and laugh a lot. They have sex. He cheats on her. She listens to bad love songs and eats cookies. She gets his best friend, played by the even hotter Colin Firth, to cook dinner for her, and then they make out in the rain and fall in love. Roll the credits.

First of all, in just about every romantic movie, the main characters have unlimited sex with absolutely no consequences whatsoever. Yes, there are breakups, but there are always make-ups. The movie never ends with the lead female character alone and crying, pregnant, or with some venereal disease. No way. Even if a woman gets pregnant in the movies, she leaves the city and moves home with her parents. Or there is an emotional scene at the airport after the father of the child fights traffic to get there and stop the plane and tell her he does love her after all and he wants to make it work. They laugh and kiss. Roll the credits.

Ladies, this is not reality. I would love to tell you it is. But as much as I've tried to make movie heroes out of my real-life boyfriends, it NEVER WORKS. There are several differences between movie romances and real life:

1. In movie romances the lines are scripted, so the characters always have a witty comeback or tender poem to recite at a moment's notice. The professional writers tell them what to say all the time. In real life we're usually so mad or nervous that we end up garbling our words, and it's an emotional mess. Sometimes we talk with our mouths full and we spit on someone.

2. Men and women in the movies have personal trainers, makeup and hair artists, and Hollywood lighting to

make them look flawless. They have absolutely no body fat, and costume designers pick out the most flattering [and expensive] clothes possible. These characters don't spill ketchup on themselves before a big date unless there is some comedic magic to follow the event. These people have editors to make sure every moment of their romance is flawlessly portrayed. They have no acne or bald spots because those get edited out. They are perfect in every way.

3. Characters in the movies have the magic of movie money. They can plan elaborate dates, including trips to Europe, or have the band play their "special" song at just the right moment. The hero in the movie can ask his future fiancée's friendly boss and entire family to quit work for a day and be a part of his magical, musical marriage proposal with fireworks included. In real life this would break most guys' bank accounts. But in the movies money is never an object. Everything is free, and it all works out in the end to make the girl so happy she cries. Men in movies don't just buy roses; they buy the whole flower store and have it delivered.

4. Men in the movies are great dancers. Some of them are trained, and others just seem to have that keen ability to tango at a moment's notice. Some of them — like my favorite, Patrick Swayze — have sexy music playing in their apartments at all times. When a woman enters, this type of guy grabs her and immediately dips her oh so perfectly. Then the music fades and they enter into a musical kissing moment, still danc-

ing while he begins to remove items of her clothing. He then wakes her up with roses and breakfast in bed and starts talking about how he's "never felt like this before." They eventually dance some more and end up together with her dad's approval. At the end they do some sort of grand-finale lift!

Yes, Ron knew I was obsessed with *Dirty Dancing*, and he was very aware that I wanted to be "Baby in the corner" more than life itself. So he took it upon himself to take dance lessons so we could dance to the theme song "Time of My Life" and do the lift at our wedding. So, yes, there are exceptions to every rule, and fairy tales can come true. It's just more comedic in real life when the guy pulls out his back in dance rehearsal a week before the wedding and skins his knee when he tries to crawl on the floor like the guy in the movie. But he got an A+ for effort and I love him for it. But let me also say, with God as my witness, that he has never had music playing in our house upon my entering, nor has he ever danced with me in our living room, dipping me in a sultry way. The closest we ever got to that was his singing karaoke in my ear via his karaoke machine. He did his best Elvis impersonations all night, but that was about it.

PLAY GAMES
[Twister is the only game that will get you any love]

If there is one thing we women are champions at, it's playing games. I'm not talking about Monopoly, but rather the kind of mind games that have been driving men insane for centuries. If you want to ruin your dating life, the best thing to do is be dishonest and play mind games with every guy you date.

Listen, I know we learn in magazine articles not to show our true emotions too soon. Those magazines give a bunch of advice on how to gain the upper hand in a relationship, how to be the lead partner in this dance we call dating. But seriously, who is writing this stuff? I think it's making us crazier than ever. Why do we women think adding drama to a relationship is going to be a good thing? It's always good in theory, isn't it? But dating is hard enough already. We certainly don't need the crash and burn of a dramatic fallout on account of sloppy game playing.

What is this theory that we're supposed to be open but not too open, aloof but not cold? The experts are always using these dumb adjectives to teach us ladies how to behave with men to get them to do what we want, as if they are trained dogs. There is even a book out there about how to train any man by using the same principles as training a dog. So do we want a boyfriend or a pet? I say stop the madness and be real with the poor guy. He's trying; he really is. Do you want him to play mind games with you, toying with your emotions just to see if he can? No! Then don't do it to him. It's not nice.

I know a lot of us play these mind games with men

subconsciously because, deep inside, we're trying to protect ourselves from getting hurt. Yes, that is a valid concern. But there are better ways to go about saving face [and heartache]. I'm not suggesting you spill your guts and divulge every thought and desire you have before your third date. But you also don't need to pretend you're busy when he asks you out because you don't want to seem too available. Or manipulate information to spend more time with him. Or sneakily check his text-message inbox to find out what he does when he's not with you. Or any of the other insane things we women do to make things go our way!

I know there are guys reading this chapter who are in disbelief that women actually think these things up. Listen, boys, there are more of us crazies out there than you think. Be afraid; be very afraid. But at least I'm writing this to help women out there see how absolutely ridiculous this behavior is.

We girls often treat dating like a tennis match, where every action is worth a certain number of points:

- If he calls the day after a date, plus two points.
- If he calls and doesn't leave a message, minus one point.
- If he doesn't call for three days, minus three points.
- If you call him instead, minus three points for you.
- If he calls and leaves a message and you call him back, it's a tie.

Okay, maybe we don't come right out and use scorecards, but believe me, we do count every day that goes by until the guy calls. The phone thing tends to be very important in determining where we stand in the relationship. Of course, there's also e-mail, which adds another element of confusion to the game. Basically, it's a cop-out for guys who don't want to pick up the phone — LAME.

Girls, I know what you're thinking. So many times in relationships, guys come on so strongly and sweep us off our feet, and then when they officially have us, they freak out and disappear into the sunset. But — and I know this requires trust — you can't think that every guy is going to be like that. Some men out there actually have good intentions to get to know you and pursue something meaningful. Playing with their minds and hearts through manipulation, score keeping, and secrets will not alleviate this problem but rather will make things more difficult for you. We all know that playing games is just another form of trying to keep a guy from running away, but believe me, if the guy is going to run, he's going to do so whether or not you play games.

I don't have some secret formula for how not to play games when you're getting to know a new person. But I know this: If you're interested in a guy, it's okay to let him know. Don't blow off his calls or make up little lies to seem aloof. If you're not interested in a guy, it's okay to let him know that, too. Don't string him along because you think it's fun or because it's flattering to your ego. That's not cool.

Seriously, examine your motives and pray to God for wisdom. Try to be as honest and real as you can because that's what you'd expect out of the guy, right? Save the games for the field and try something different: straight-up honesty and integrity. You both might just win in the end.

Okay, so on that note, I will conclude section 2 of this book. Section 3 is for you boys! And having dated quite a few of you, I suggest you read it very carefully.

THE MEN'S DEPARTMENT: AND I'M NOT TALKING ABOUT SQUARE FOOTAGE AT SEARS

CAN I HAVE YOUR ATTENTION?

Welcome.

As you might have suspected, since Kerri wrote the majority of the women's section, I (Matthew) am here to guide you through the final section of this book, with a little help from Kerri. And not surprising, it's all about some of the issues a lot of Christian men encounter while dating. But Kerri said her women's section is for both genders, and the same is true here; just because this section is for the guys, I very much recommend that women read it too. However, I've attempted to write with the average guy in mind, which means you will notice some slight differences in section 3:

- The information is a little interactive, for those of you who are attention deficit.

- A lot of the content is in bulleted points, for those of you who are attention deficit.

Speaking of attention deficit, that overused term brings us to a good first point about dating: Your dating life might be more successful if the women you dated didn't have to work so hard at holding your attention. Most of you know exactly what I'm talking about. Believe it or not [and unfortunately for us attention-deficit people], women [in addition to many household pets] enjoy having your undivided attention once in a while. And, of course, a large part of attention means listening. I'm sure, however, that you are already aware that listening is an important part of any romantic relationship.

That's right; according to relationship expert Imfwama Wotela, paying attention is one of the ten most essential ingredients to a happy and fulfilling relationship. "Be attentive when your partner is speaking," writes Wotela. "Watch their expressions and learn to know their gestures too so that you are able to read their actions easily."* Since it's often said that a guy hears his boss, bud, and bro better than he hears his girlfriend, Imfwama's advice might be a little difficult to accomplish, even more so than pronouncing her name.

But in spite of our having a dickens of a time paying attention to the opposite sex once in a while, that's no excuse not to pay attention to this section. So, gentlemen, lend me your ears for a moment, and you might learn a thing or two about what you're doing right or wrong or not at all when dating.

---

* Imfwama Wotela, "Ingredients of Happy Relationships: Mix Them Together for Results," *LuvCube*, http://www.luvcube.com/live-love/happy-relationships-ingredients.htm.

MR. NICE GUY HAS A FEW ISSUES

You're probably a good guy. I mean, sure, you have your issues [we all have them], but nonetheless, you're not a bad person. A good percentage of Christian guys — at least the ones I know — are good people. And, yes, I am aware that according to Jesus, *no one is truly good but God*, and I believe that, but I also think you know what I mean: I'm simply talking about our earthly perspective of good. But dating — that is, the kind we do inside the church — sometimes does a number on the good Christian male. Like you, I have encountered a lot of challenges firsthand.

Most people — those who know me personally, anyway — consider me to be a pretty nice guy. Again, that's *most* people; there are certainly a few who wouldn't agree with that sentiment. In fact, those people might even say that I am mean, coldhearted, and sometimes manipulative. Furthermore, most of those people can be found in my ex-girlfriends group. And believe me, that's not something I'm proud of. In fact, it makes me sad. But the really sad part is that there's very little I can do about it. It's not like now that I am thirty-three, married, and perhaps a bit wiser in my understanding of relationships I can go back to all the girls I have dated in the past and say, "Hey! Remember me? Yeah, I was just in the neighborhood and I wanted to stop by and tell you that you were right: I was a really bad boyfriend! Will you forgive me?" At least one of them would probably slap me in the face.

I know dating is hard for us guys, but I'm not willing to make that our excuse. However, I am pointing out that, for whatever reason, dating does tend to bring out the worst in us.

For many of us Christian males, no other facet of life — except maybe a family reunion when you're playing badminton with your uncle Ted, who is, quite frankly, an idiot — brings out the worst in our personalities more than when we're in pursuit of a member of the female species. For guys — and, like Kerri points out, for women too — dating is just that one thing that can turn even the nicest of us into the biggest of jerks. And in addition to being a jerk, we can also become emotional, needy, angry, stubborn, dumb, anxious, and the list goes on to include spontaneous, narcissistic, selfish, codependent, awkward, and, at times, a wee bit psychotic.

Dang. Ouch, right? Unless you like being that guy, I'm sure that last sentence stung a bit. Believe me, it wasn't that much fun to write, either. Now that I am looking at those words all bunched up together in one sentence, it sounds like that person — um, on occasion, *me* — shouldn't be allowed to walk around in public. And according to the women I spoke to in the process of writing this book, I am not alone in my struggles. Most girls told me not just one story but two, three, or more about the horrendous dating experiences they had with Christian guys. Some of the stories were quite extreme. Think about this one from thirty-three-year-old Karen:

> Michael was my friend for almost five years. During the first four years our friendship was strictly platonic. Then one day, the day before I turned twenty-nine, out of the blue he declared his feelings for me. Michael was one of the nicest guys I knew; I sincerely loved him. His words were heartfelt, and since I had always been a little

interested, I told him I was willing to entertain the idea of us being in a relationship with one another. Our parents were thrilled; my mom and dad had always like Michael. "He just seems like such a godly young man," Mom would say to me.

For two months we dated, and quite honestly, it was great. I had become convinced that there was a real possibility that he and I would end up married. But sixty-seven days into our relationship, all of that changed. While out to eat with a couple of friends, I noticed that something was severely bothering him. "I don't think I can date you anymore," he said after we were alone in the car. "This isn't working for me." Now, I knew our relationship wasn't perfect, but we hadn't experienced anything out of the ordinary. "Why isn't this working for you, Michael?" I asked. He couldn't give me a reason; he just looked off into the distance with an expression on his face that I had never seen before. "Michael, this isn't you," I said. "What's wrong, baby?" His only response to me was, "You're not right for me." That was the last thing he said to me when he dropped me off at my apartment. The next day he called me, which surprised me, really; I didn't expect to hear from him, at least not that soon. He apologized to me and told me he didn't mean anything he had said. I was hesitant to let him back in so easily, but he cried, and so, rather stupidly, I took him back.

TIPS: BREAKING UP IS HARD TO DO

[but it doesn't have to be as bad as we make it]

Okay, so relationships don't always work out, guys. But just because this is true doesn't mean you have to go through a *bad* breakup. Sometimes, because one or both of you are acting like idiots, the bad breakup is unavoidable. But if you follow this advice, it might not be quite as bad:

- **Tell her first.** It's only fair. I mean, she is the one who has put up with you all this time, so buck up, guys, and don't tell the world your plan until you've told her.

- **Do it in person.** Not over the phone, not in an e-mail or text message, and not in a letter! In person! Grow a pair! The least you can do is have the courtesy to tell her your thoughts face-to-face.

- **Don't expect it to be easy.** Even if deep down she thinks you're a total jerk, she's probably going to cry [mainly because she's not breaking up with you first]. And, hey, you might cry too.

- **Talk to her on her playing field.** Don't make her drive home after you boot her out of your house. Allow her to go straight to bed to cry some more.

- **Be honest.** If you've fallen out of love with her, tell her that. Sure, it's not a pretty story, but you're breaking up, remember? The story isn't pretty.

- **Don't be mean.** This is not the time to get everything you ever wanted to say to her off your chest. Just cut to the chase.

- **Help her see your point of view.** And in the end, if she still doesn't get it, just tell her, "Well, I don't feel like I have to keep explaining myself over and over again."

- **Don't leave it up in the air.** If you're going to end it, END IT! Very few couples who frequently break up and get back together again truly end up working out. Some do, but most do not! Oh, and don't change your mind.

- **Don't call her the next day.** She'll be fine. I promise. Separation is good.

- **Kiss her good-bye only if the mood is right.** Don't end a big fight with a kiss. Use your kisses sparingly and unselfishly, not to get your last final kick with her. And *definitely* don't make out with her after you break up. That's what they call a mixed message.

- **Stay in control of the moment.** Set up a time limit that you think is appropriate. After that time is up, just tell her you have to go.

Karen's e-mail to me went on to describe a very bumpy six months. Not only did Michael's personality become more and more inconsistent, but Karen became obsessed with trying to help him. And according to Karen, he eventually became emotionally abusive. She finally found the strength to break away from the relationship. One of the saddest things she wrote to me was this: "I literally felt like I had been through a war." Obviously, Karen had numerous questions, not the least of which were these:

- Did Michael ever really love me?
- Had he ever put other girls through this emotional roller coaster?
- Was he sick? Or was he simply unsure of his feelings for me?

- Was he *really* a good guy?

All of those questions are difficult — if not impossible — to answer. However, though Karen's was by far one of the most drastic stories I was told while writing this book, it was not the only bad one. The stories I heard from girls about us Christian guys included:

- Horrible, freakish breakups
- Guys who were unable to hear the word *no*
- Overwhelming guilt from past relationships
- Verbal abuse
- Mood swings
- Codependence
- Jealousy

Almost every girl said that before they began dating, as far as they could tell the guys were amazing *godly* men. But do they sound like great guys? Okay, I don't mean to sound judgmental; who's to say they weren't great guys? But who's to say they were?

So here's the big question: Why does dating bring out the worst in us? [And, no, it's not true for every guy, but it's true for a lot of us.] I suppose you might be able to say that it is one of the million-dollar questions, on the same scale or magnitude as these:

- Why do bad things happen to good people?
- Why did God create Satan?

- Why is Paris Hilton famous?

And, of course, like all the big questions that have boggled humanity since the beginning of time, or at least since the beginning of the Modern Age, people have certainly offered many answers to the dating question. That's been especially true since the 1980s, when we as a culture became convinced that we were so much more clever than our ancestors, mainly because we were able to not only calculate the human psyche using various tests and diagnostics but also display our results using pie charts! Since then, a lot of very intelligent people have come up with some pretty good answers to that question. And while some of the answers have helped us with many of our relational woes, such as allowing us to evolve from our tendencies to be like apes in a china shop when it comes to our dating behavior, the experts have hardly solved the entire equation or developed some miracle formula. Let's face it: If there were a magic potion, a lot of women would force their men — husbands, boyfriends, friends with benefits, and/or guys they're interested in learning more about — to drink it down fast.

But don't begin to think there is no hope for you. If you're a guy who thinks of himself as dating impaired, you're hardly alone. And truthfully, unless you have never experienced any kind of healthiness or success in a relationship, you're probably not as bad off as you might think. Or as the case might be, you're probably not as bad off as others — meaning the girls you've dated or liked or stalked — would suggest. Are you perfect? Heavens no! But you're probably not insane, or at least the chances are good that you're not so insane that you can't have a successful relationship.

Before we jump into the nitty-gritty of the content, consider these questions:*

- Do you consider any of your past relationships a success?
- What do you believe was the core reason for their success or failure?
- What is your biggest fear when it comes to dating?
- If you were to find the right person, would marriage be something you would be ready to pursue?
- Do you have any issues you know are interfering with your dating life?

SUCCESSFUL AND HEALTHY
[YOU WANT THIS WHEN YOU'RE DATING]

Okay, so let me ask you another question: Are you interested in a dating life? Yeah, maybe the answer to that question is obvious, considering that you're reading a book about dating, and those uninterested in dating don't usually read dating books. So perhaps I should phrase the question this way: Are you interested in having a *successful* and *healthy* dating life? Your answer should be just as obvious. But before you stumble around trying

---

* Ladies, these questions might be good ones to remember when you're drinking coffee, looking very coy, and trying to get to know that special guy sitting across from you.

to form your answer into sentences, let me explain what I mean. Being successful and healthy doesn't necessarily mean this:

- You're ready to jump into marriage as soon as you find the right girl.
- You're going to be perfect and never make a mistake or break someone's heart. Believe me, it's bound to happen.

Having a successful and healthy dating lifestyle actually means this:

- You're not haphazardly dating because you're a little lonely or horny.
- You're not looking for a relationship with a woman to fulfill you or complete you.
- Your dating life has a sense of purpose.

Back when I was in high school and contemplating dating, one of my non-insane youth pastors said to me, "Matthew, when you begin dating, please don't be a moron." Those were simple words — and honestly, I think they were in reference to his insane wife — but looking back, I am inclined to think they were also very good words. "Don't be a moron!" Hopefully that's what you want to do — avoid being a complete idiot when it comes to dating! Again, just in case you haven't heard me say this the last twenty times, that's not to say you won't make mistakes — you're bound to make a few — but the goal of healthy and successful dating is to avoid the more obvious

AN IM CONVERSATION WITH TWENTY-TWO-YEAR-OLD JOE, CURRENTLY A YOUTH PASTOR

Matthew: In your opinion, what's the most frustrating part about dating as a Christian guy?

Joe: I would say it's probably the whole "spiritual leader" thing. A lot of Christian girls say they're looking for a spiritual leader in a relationship, but no one knows what that really means. Some girls end up dating guys who are total jerks most of the time, but because they pray together every night, they somehow get manipulated into thinking the way they're treated is okay. On the other hand, I know girls who have dated great guys, but because the guys don't do Bible studies with them every night, they get mad. Sometimes you think you can't win!

Matthew: At what age did you have your first serious relationship?

Joe: Seventeen.

Matthew: Looking back, would you classify it as a healthy relationship?

Joe: No, not healthy at all!

Matthew: How so?

Joe: Eh, it was one of those things. She was a cute Christian girl, so I thought that's all we needed. But throughout our entire relationship, all we did was drag each other down.

We got way too physical, and by the time it was over, things had gone so far that I thought I was obligated to marry her.

Matthew: Really? Okay, I won't ask. Joe, had your church's youth leader talked to you about dating?

Joe: Not really. Of course, everyone talked about Joshua Harris, but our youth leader encouraged us to date.

Matthew: How did your relationship end?

Joe: It didn't end well. I guess I grew out of it eventually and was ready for it to be over. We'd broken up and gotten back together several times. But one day I ended it for good. We didn't talk for a long, long time after that, and we're still not friends. In the end, she deeply resented me for it and ended up in a few bad relationships after that.

Matthew: Do you wish you had never dated that girl? Or do you believe the lessons learned made it worth it?

Joe: If I thought the only way we could learn not to sin was by sinning first, then I wouldn't believe in the power of the Holy Spirit. I believe that God gets us to certain places and teaches us certain lessons. We get there either the easy way or the hard way.

pitfalls of dating, the ones where hearts get beat up and ugly scars prevail.

And your reputation gets utterly shafted.

But here's where it might get a little difficult: To avoid moron status, you're going to have to embrace some relational maturity. I know that seems farfetched and boring, but don't worry: That doesn't mean you have to toss out your PS3 [mostly because I know the chances of that happening are about as likely as Nerf making a comeback] and become an adult overnight. But embracing some maturity might very well mean that you have to engage in a certain type of thinking about how you pursue relationships with the opposite sex, which, quite honestly, shouldn't be all that shocking to you. I mean, you are more than likely "of age" — old enough to vote, buy tobacco, and legally google pictures of naked women on the Internet — so I think it's only fair that you know how to date with a little intelligence and care.

Seem like a feasible concept?

 QUESTIONS TO CONSIDER:

- What does dating success mean to you?
- How would you define healthy dating?

ONLINE DATING TIPS

[by Kerri]

1. Never sign on to any dating site:
   a. after running into your ex and her new fiancé.
   b. after one in the morning.
   c. after watching any film starring Brad Pitt, Tom Cruise, or Russell Crowe.
2. Do not put in your profile that your interests include long walks on the beach if you reside in Ohio or another such state.
3. If you list *Fried Green Tomatoes* as your favorite movie to appear more in touch with your feminine side, it would be a good idea to actually have seen the movie or at least know one of the stars. And don't list *Beaches* because then we *know* you're lying.
4. Glamour head shots featuring stage makeup and halo lighting do not make you look sexy! You may get a response like, "Nice head shot . . . are you wearing makeup?"
5. If asked what you are looking for in a mate, a good response is an honest one, such as, "Someone who is willing to lie about how we met." Honesty is so important. Or if asked what you'd like to do on a first date, an appropriate response might be, "Well, we met online, so I'd like to go to the police station to get fingerprinted." Remember, be open. Someone may be in prison now, but think how much time he or she has to read the Bible and other great works of literature. Seriously, though, honesty [and a little humility] is the best policy for online dating. If you really are looking to find your mate, then implying you're better than you are will only make you look worse in the long run.

MOTIVES

Many of the mistakes guys make when dating come down to their motives. In other words, why are you dating? Knowing the answer to that question can often help guys avoid some of the more obvious errors in dating. As is often the case, many guys don't really have a defined answer to that question until they've stumbled a few times and left a trail of awful dating experiences behind them.

Like I talked about at the beginning of this book, most people date with "me" in mind. Most guys [and girls, for that matter] have good reason to enter the dating world holding the "me" card. Why? Well, it's mostly because of the experiences in their past:

- They have a jaded view of male/female relationships that stems from observing their parents.
- They have been hurt before, and it's taking everything they've got to get up and try again.
- They haven't dated before.

People's motives are an important part of what defines them. And, like much of what Jesus speaks about in the Gospels, our motives are connected with what is going on inside our hearts. If we enter the dating scene with messed-up motives, we run the risk of ruining our dating lives.

QUESTIONS TO CONSIDER:

- What are your dating motives?
- What determines or has determined your motives?
- How does having a pure heart play a role in your dating life? [Hint: It's not simply about sex.]

ARE YOU *WASTING* TIME?

[blunt advice for the total slackers]

This might be *way* too obvious, but if you're into getting wasted, whether it be from alcohol* or drugs or compulsive gambling or obsessive video-game playing, then you are probably not mature enough to pursue a serious relationship with the opposite sex. I'm sorry; is that too harsh? Maybe it is. Well, you're tough; you can handle it. If this is you, you're probably the Christian rebel who can take a little beating anyway. You're the type of guy a lot of girls would like to date. That's cool and all, but often, despite your lack of respect for yourself, you further complicate the issue by leading nice [but naive] girls into your little world of whacked-out destruction. [Okay, so maybe "whacked-out destruction" is too dramatic, but you know what I mean.] Sure, she's fully capable of making her own decisions. But do not underestimate the power of your influence. And because a lot of girls are intrigued by guys with devilish charm [something that, if kept in check, can really help you], all it takes are a few kind words and empty promises combined with built-in sex appeal, and you can woo her into your little world rather easily.

---

* I just want to clarify that I don't believe alcohol is a problem *if you're a responsible human being*. But if you're prone to abusing alcohol or you're drinking only so you can get drunk and act like a complete fool, that's a problem. Sure, a lot of us have made mistakes — but mistakes are one thing and habits are quite another.

So with that rather snottily written paragraph in mind, consider the following:

- **Your life is your life.** You can do whatever you want with the time God has given you, and that means that if you find enjoyment in being wasted, who am I to tell you you're a complete idiot? So please, go ahead and find some kind of encouragement in what I just said.

- **But if you're serious about following Jesus — and, yes, you've heard this before — you know that your life is *not* really your own.** Yeah, that's not my thinking — that would be the apostle Paul's. So you might want to rethink your habits, especially in light of wanting to eventually marry a girl with morals. Hey, it's just a thought.

- **Your habits are a reflection of you.** You probably know this, too! If a girl truly cares about herself and her relationship with God, she'll take into consideration your habits.

- **She can't save you.** Don't let her try.

- **Don't introduce bad habits to her even if she wants you to.** Even if you have a habit of going out and getting wasted on the weekends, prove you're still a decent guy by *not* taking a girl down with you.

WHAT YOU AS A GUY CAN DO TO RUIN YOUR DATING LIFE

DATE JUST TO HOOK UP

I don't believe that most Christian guys walk into a room full of people, whether it be a bar or a singles' group, and think to themselves, *Hmmm, who can I score with tonight?* I'm sure some Christians do that, but the vast majority of us don't. That's not to say dating just to hook up doesn't happen among Christians; it does. It happens all the time.

Usually this kind of behavior begins with an unmet need — for a Christian guy, that need is often companionship, physical attention, or just something supposedly mysterious and exciting. I also think that because many of us have been raised in sheltered environments, we often desire to see what "the other side of trouble" looks like.

When I was in college, I lived two distinct lives. Eighty-five percent of the time, I was the guy who went to church, told people about Jesus, and was known as the "good kid." I spent the other 15 percent of my time trying to explore all the things I'd never experienced and had heard so much about. Balancing that life, as you may know, is quite difficult; I wanted to explore, but I also wanted to do it without messing up the other 85 percent of me — or at least without getting caught.

Finding a random hookup within my Christian circles was less difficult than I imagined it would be. My boyish good looks [if I do say so myself] and the fact that I was nice to everyone [to their face] often served me well. On a couple of occasions, I met a girl who was just like me — sweet, innocent, and looking for that ambiguous "something." Neither of us was interested in dating necessarily [at least that's what we said], yet when we were alone — having coffee, pretending to study, or just having a conversation — we flirted. And about two seconds after we had met, the relationship/friendship/whatever got physical. [I'll leave the details out.]

I remember after one of these interactions, I walked a girl to her car at about two a.m. That was the last time I saw her. Oh, she called the next day, but somewhere between two and eleven a.m., 13 percent of my 15 percent found Jesus again, so I ignored her call. She wrote me e-mails, wondering what was up with me. I never responded, my conscience not allowing me to. About six weeks later, I got my last e-mail from her, and it was a doozy. She told me she couldn't believe I had treated her just like every non-Christian guy she had ever met.

Other Christian guys have confessed to me their stories about hookups or one-night stands, and a lot of them happened much like the story I just told. But here's a really sad reality: None of the guys I talked to said anything about the effects their little adventure had on the girl. In fact, most of them talked about her as if she were just a small part of the story line. Believe me, I am not judging; I have done the same thing. Because of the spiritual implications of making a mistake like that, I concentrated only on what was going on in my own heart and mind.

Consider Katie's story:

I am twenty-five years old; I have been a Christian for almost seventeen years, and up until January 1, 2006,

I was a virgin. I was at a friend's New Year's Eve party, and while hanging out in the hot tub, I met Christopher [twenty-eight years old]. Almost instantly, Christopher and I hit it off. We talked for hours. As people left the party, we were still in our bathing suits, chatting about everything from work to church to past relationships. Later, when Christopher said good-bye to me, he kissed me. I almost melted. The next day he called me, and we ended up spending the better part of New Year's Day together. By the evening, we were back at my house, making out, giggling, and eventually pulling each other's clothes off. It's hard to even write this down, but that night, Christopher and I had sex. I knew it was wrong; for starters, I hardly knew him. In addition to that, we were both Christians. The weirdest part of the whole ordeal is that I spoke to him only two times after that, and that was over the phone. It wasn't like I didn't try to contact him; I did, but he wouldn't pick up my calls. I tried calling him every day for two weeks. On January 16, I got a text message that said, "I made a mistake; I am sorry. We can't see each other anymore."

Unless you've experienced something similar to this situation, it's probably difficult for you to imagine the pain this causes. It's one thing to lose your virginity to someone you love who then leaves you, but to lose something that has been so important to you to someone you don't even know is horrible. For the last year, I've been in therapy just so I can get over the guilt I have felt. And I have to be honest: Sometimes I wonder if he ever, even for a moment, stops and thinks to himself, *I wonder how she's doing.*

So before you go hooking up with a stranger, someone you've known only a few days, or a friend you know you might score benefits with without the bother of emotional attachment, remember that the mistake you're making affects more than just you; it affects her, too, maybe even more deeply. Also, get professional help for those needs you might be attempting to fill with a hookup.

 ## QUESTIONS TO CONSIDER:

- Have you ever experienced a random hookup?
- If so, have you ever wondered how it affected the other person?
- Do you think that because we spend so much time talking about the importance of sexual purity in our churches, the effects of a random hookup on a Christian might be greater than on a non-Christian?
- How do you manage or overcome guilt? Do you even have any?

HOLD CLOSELY TO GUILT ABOUT YOUR *LAST* HOOKUP

[and completely alienate your current relationship prospect]

Christian guys carry around a lot of guilt, especially when it comes to sex. If you've been raised in the evangelical world, you know how much emphasis is put on being sexually pure. Because of all of the time we spend discussing it in church, it's easy to see why so many Christian guys experience an overwhelming amount of guilt when they make mistakes in relationships.

IS DATING OUT OF STYLE? MAYBE.

College students are, according to a recent report by FoxNews.com, more likely to simply hook up than date. The reason? "The fear of commitment and exclusive relationships among college students may be a cause of a delayed maturation effect," says psychologist Diana Kirschner. "College-age individuals are acting more like [high schoolers] these days."*

Unfortunately, for some of you reading this book, that last section about hookups came just a little too late to be of any use to you. And, yes, that stinks, but you can't dwell on it and become overwhelmed by your mistakes. Guilt is difficult to overcome, especially when it's the religious kind. But you can overcome it, and to be truly functional, you must. Healthy and successful dating requires that you heal from guilt.

Consider the words of these young men:

---

* Marianne Lebedinskaya, "College 'Hook-Ups' Replace Dating," *FoxNews.com*, September 5, 2006, http://www.foxnews.com/story/0,2933,212207,00.html?sPage=fnc.college101.

- "I had sex with my last girlfriend, so, yeah, I dealt with guilt. It's funny, but I didn't really feel guilty until after we had broken up." Joshua, 26
- "Guilt?" [Laughs] "Isn't that like a prerequisite of relationships between Christians?" Dawson, 22
- "Do you want to hear something sad? I still sometimes feel guilty over what I did while I was dating, and I am married." Craig, 29

I can't tell you how many bad breakups I have seen happen between Christian couples over the years because the guy was unable to overcome the flaws of his sexual or relational past. As Christians, it's often the baggage we carry from a previous relationship that ends up being the cause of pain or frustration in [and hence, the breakup of] a current dating relationship. Isn't that sad? Many Christians end up not being able to truly experience their current dating relationship because of the guilt they're feeling from the last one.

I probably don't have to tell you this, but until you're over a former relationship — which means the guilt's behind you too — you don't need to be seriously dating someone new. But that's not the only thing you should know; keep the following in mind too:

- **If you're dating someone new, it means you've decided to move on.** And she's not a part of your healing process. If for some reason you haven't moved on, then get help!
- **Guilt is not attractive.** I don't know why, but sometimes

Christians carry guilt around like it's a badge of honor, like it's a necessity for working through the junk of our past. If this is you, stop trying to be overly spiritual. Remember this: If you've asked God for his forgiveness, he's forgiven you, so move on. And if you can't overcome it through prayer and meditation, then ask for help. You don't have to walk the guilt journey alone. And holding on to even a sliver of it will undoubtedly have negative effects on your future relationships.

- **Your guilt might be misplaced.** Keep in mind that the guilt you feel about past relationships might be rooted in something other than your, um, relationships. Our emotional and spiritual struggles are often caused by what we experienced as children or at church, or perhaps they are a result of a mental unbalance of some kind. So again, and this will be the last time I say this — in this section, anyway — don't walk alone; get help!

Once you realize all that it cost God to forgive you,
you will be held as in a vise, constrained by
the love of God.
OSWALD CHAMBERS, *MY UTMOST FOR HIS HIGHEST*

Fall in Love with Yourself
[the best way to make lots of girls disgusted with you]

When some guys enter the "dating pool" with ugly motives, they wade around the scene with impure and selfish tendencies, and many realities occur, including one that is like a terrorist attack on your dating life: the falling-in-love-with-yourself syndrome. More than likely you've met this guy. Though he is "faith based" and seemingly intent on keeping his heart, mind, and soul centered on godly principles, it's still hard for me to understand why any girl would fall for the guy who is in love with himself.

Yep, Christian guys can be the center of their own universes too. Just ask Christian girls about the stereotypical traits of a churchy guy who thinks he's the *total end*:

- "He usually likes his hair almost as much as his ability to quote 1 Timothy." Amanda, 25
- "Oh yeah, the church is full of guys who think they're just a little *lower than the angels* compared to everyone else; they usually have this attitude that's somewhere between Charlie Sheen and Ashton Kutcher." Cynthia, 29
- "He acts godly when he's onstage with a guitar in his hands. But really, he just likes being onstage with a guitar in his hands." Sammi, 24

Guys, let's face it: Sometimes we think more highly of ourselves than we ought to — heck, I've been there, and sometimes

I *still* suffer from it a bit. And since I live in Nashville — home of the Christian music scene [I guess there's still a Christian music scene] — I see it all the time. I'm not sure if every Christian guy who suffers from a "me complex" actually means to, but we do just the same. In addition to that, we sometimes give off the vibe that everyone else should be sick with "me" envy. And from what I've heard from listening to all the women I spoke to in relation to this book, self-absorption is always ugly on a guy.

Now, I know there's seemingly a very fine line between pride and self-confidence, but someone who possesses a little self-confidence is not focused on himself; he just believes in the man God made him to be. A man who is self-centered, on the other hand, *loves* giving the credit to himself and actually looks for opportunities to do so. It probably doesn't hurt to be reminded what the Bible says about Mr. Christian Idol: "Pride goes before destruction" (Proverbs 16:18), "Humble yourself before your God" (Daniel 10:12), and "Walk humbly with your God" (Micah 6:8).

In a dating relationship, the "me" guy will:

- forget to think about how his actions affect the other person. [And the last time I checked, a relationship is about always taking the other person's feelings into consideration.]
- not consider that the problem is ever him. [And trust me, it's sometimes you, far more often than you would like to think.]
- resist asking for help because he's convinced that he doesn't need any. [Someday you will wake up and

realize that you do need help, but until then, try not to hurt anybody with that large plank in your eye.]
- be unable to see just how undateable he really is. [Others see it, but you can't.]

Look in the mirror. I mean, you probably enjoy doing that anyway, so go ahead and do it again. Ask God to show you a glimpse of how your motive of serving "me" is hurting your ability to build strong relationships. Ask him to show you the areas in your life where humility is needed. To be honest, the core issue is pride, and pride is a battle you will be fighting for the rest of your life [whether you're married or not]. So don't think that just because you're experiencing a successful relationship, you don't have a problem with focusing a little too much on "me."

 ## QUESTIONS TO CONSIDER:

- In your opinion, how does self-centeredness affect a relationship?
- How does one begin to learn the practice of thinking *less* of himself?
- What does humility mean in a dating relationship?

RESIST COMMITMENT
[like it's the plague]

Ugh. Just reading the word *commitment* makes some of you become subject to headaches. Oh, I know, *commitment* is just one of those words that can cause even the best of us guys to shake in our boots.

Of course, some of you are braver than others. However, even if you don't believe you fear commitment, more than likely you understand how a guy could become a bit overwhelmed by the weight of the "c-word." But you really must know this: Resisting commitment [with the right woman] will wreak havoc on your dating life.

If you're serious about dating, you probably should be dating with commitment in mind. It's not like you have to be ready to jump into a tux and scurry down the aisle as quickly as Britney and Kevin, but if you are seriously interested in dating with the right motives, you should be *ready* to commit when the time is right.

Nonetheless, a lot of guys fear it. Why do you think that is? Well, according to AskMen.com,* there are many reasons:

- Loss of personal freedom
- Loss of personal space
- One sexual partner forever
- Burned before

---

* Matthew Fitzgerald, "Why We're Afraid of Commitment," *AskMen.com*, http://www. askmen.com/dating/curtsmith_100/131_dating_advice.html.

- Emotional baggage
- Loss of free time
- Just not ready for it
- Resist trusting women

While the average Christian guy would probably state his reasons for fearing commitment a little differently than those [hopefully at least one or two of them, but, hey, maybe not], they probably aren't as untrue as we would like them to be. I think the idea of commitment can make us feel a bit trapped, especially when it happens with the wrong woman.

For me, and also for a lot of Christian guys I know, commitment doesn't become scary until we've actually committed. I'm not sure about you, but when I was in the midst of the dating scene, I wanted to commit. In fact, I was probably a little "commitment happy." It all started when I was in my mid-twenties and it seemed like all my friends were getting married or had serious girlfriends. Every wedding I attended would leave me feeling less and less like a complete individual. And sadly, on at least three different occasions, I jumped into a relationship just because I desired commitment. It felt okay for a month or two, but eventually I started feeling stifled and cramped, kind of like I was suffocating.

Does that sound familiar? Have you ever been in a relationship where you believed you were about ready to suffocate? It's not like I would enter the commitment knowing it wouldn't work out; believe me, I wanted it to work out. But it wouldn't, mainly because I would freak out and call the whole thing off shortly after it had begun. However, the reason these relationships didn't work was that my motives were still very much flawed.

What were my motives for dating? Well, at the time, I just wanted to *feel* like I was on the verge of experiencing marital bliss. I wanted to *not* feel so out of place when I was hanging around all my friends who were getting together two-by-two like they were about to board Noah's ark. I wanted to feel the companionship of a woman, her touch, her beauty. Frankly, I wanted to get to a place where I knew that sex — the guilt-free kind — was right around the corner. So though I didn't fear the first step of commitment, once I opened my mouth and confessed my love, I began to run like a scared little kid.

Why? Because much to my frustration, I wasn't with the right woman.

You might fear commitment for very different reasons. Maybe you don't know why you're scared of commitment. Maybe all you know is that whenever you think about it, you just can't make yourself go through with it.

If this is you, it's important for you to do some self-discovery and figure out why you can't commit. Being able to commit is, for obvious reasons, I suppose, one of the most important facets to being able to pursue dating in a healthy and successful manner. Consider the following possibilities to help you get started.

- **Your parents.** Have you considered that the relation-ship between your mom and dad might have some-thing to do with it? Were they happy? Are you a child of divorce? And if so, have you ever truly dealt with that reality? Did your mom or dad have an affair?

Perhaps your parents' relationship was almost perfect and you're scared you won't be able to live up to it.

- **Your age.** Maybe you're simply not ready to even engage the thought of committing because you're only twenty years old. You can barely keep your bathroom clean, so the idea of giving your heart to one person overwhelms you with much fear and trembling.

- **Your past relationships.** Have you been hurt in a past relationship? Maybe it wasn't even a dating relationship; maybe it was a teacher or clergyman or aunt or uncle — someone you thought you could trust. Instead of finding something you could cling to, all you found was brokenness.

- **Your emotional stability.** Um, this is probably a bit overwhelming to think about, but have you ever considered the fact that maybe you've got some pretty serious emotional issues, like depression, anxiety, codependence, bipolar disorder, or something similar? Any of these issues might be playing into the fear you encounter when you even think about committing to a woman.

- **Your secret.** The truth is, you're not attracted to women and you don't know why. You're probably not ready to call yourself "gay," but you know that for some reason, ever since you were ten years old, you haven't felt the need to daydream about girls; instead you spent more time being anxious about gym class, hoping no one would notice you staring.

- **Your God-plan.** Is God keeping you from committing? Could he have something else for you? Maybe a career move? Going to the mission field? Maybe you're supposed to wait to get married until you're thirty-three, not twenty-five. Maybe he's simply protecting you from a major mistake you're about to make.

Obviously, all these factors could have nothing to do with why you're unable to make a commitment. Here's the deal: Only you know why committing scares you. I hate to break it to you, but you *need* to work through your fears before you will be able to pursue what is healthy and successful.

And with the *right* person, commitment is the most beautiful of things.

A VERSE TO REMEMBER

Because we have these promises, dear friends, let us cleanse ourselves from everything that can defile our body or spirit. And let us work toward complete holiness because we fear God. (2 Corinthians 7:1)

BE SCARY
[by Kerri]

Hello, guys. It's me again! I know, I know, you're probably crazy excited about this. I mean, Matthew's great and all, but he's a bit too serious for me. [*Hold on, boys. Please don't fall in love with me right now. I know I'm super cute, but I'm married. I'm unavailable. Great . . . you love me more now, don't you?*]

Okay, so I wanted to cover this topic because a lot of people joke about being scary, but I don't think guys truly understand how serious this problem is. Oh, I'm not kidding; there's a lot that you guys can do to scare women away. Yes, I know we girls can do the same, but I'm talking to you guys now. Just focus with me, boys. It's time you learned a thing or two about the

SOME FRANK ADVICE YOU MAY NOT WANT TO HEAR

[but I (Matthew) think you need to]

If you're thirty-five and single, college students probably don't want to date you. I mean, there's always the exception, but you shouldn't bet on exceptions. You should assume they don't want to date you unless one comes along and tells you otherwise. So with that said, stop hanging around them. You're making them feel funny — and, no, not a good funny.

If you weigh 362 pounds, the size-six girl is probably not going to give you a second glance. And that doesn't necessarily make her shallow; she's just not into you, bro. Sorry.

If you're not willing to make a few sacrifices, you're not ready for a serious relationship. Dating another person means that you might have to make a couple of sacrifices, and that's a pretty important aspect of any relationship. It's not like you should be ready to give up everything that you know to be "you," but you should be ready to give up a little something here and there.

If you think marriage means "happily ever after," you need your head examined. That's not to say it isn't amazing; I love married life. But my wife and I have to *work* at maintaining a healthy and successful married relationship. Sometimes it's fun; sometimes it's rough. But I promise it's worth it. Just make sure you get your head out of the sand.

comments you're making, especially at the beginning stages of getting to know a girl.

I'm not sure why, but some of you just blurt out whatever is on your mind without censoring yourself at all. And if you're not thinking about your comments, you will definitely end up sticking your foot in your mouth or, worse still, coming across as one of those really creepy guys. *Ick!* And, of course, there's nothing sexier to a woman than a man who makes her skin crawl or makes her want to change her phone number — *or both*. But in my opinion, if you want to scare a girl off completely, come on way too strong in the beginning.

Here are some ways to do just that:

- Begin the first date by doing genealogical research on her family and yours to make sure you're not related. Then tell her that even if you were cousins, it would be okay, because you've done it before. Then justify that comment by saying, "Well, if you think about it, we're all related to Adam and Eve, aren't we?"
- Go ahead and tell her she's sexy right at the beginning of the date. For increased fun, name specific body parts you're really attracted to and why. Compare her to other women you think are sexy, like Paris Hilton.
- Tell her you've been staring at her picture in the church directory; in fact, go ahead and admit that you've cut it out and glued it to your ceiling. Then add, "I've been praying a lot about you."
- Make lots of comments about your intentions to marry her.

Okay, enough with the nonsense. Are you getting the picture, boys? Yeah, don't be scary. We know you're nervous and sometimes overly excited to be out of the house on a date with a girl. Maybe this is your first date since the 1980s, but it's up to you to keep a somewhat composed front. Sure, we want to know you're interested, but we don't want to fear that you're going to chop us up into little pieces on the third date and then store us in your basement. You see, sometimes you guys think you're being funny, but we don't get your humor. Sarcasm is most definitely a tricky thing, and it's best left alone for at least the first few dates. Trust me, I know. I've been on your side of the fence with my sarcastic attempts at humor, and sometimes they've come off as scary.

But I think I have some help for you guys. I could say something cliché like, "Just try to be yourself," but you'd probably end up laughing at me, thinking to yourself, *Why would I want to do that? Being myself hasn't worked for me in eight years!* But you know, sooner or later you're going to have to be yourself anyway, so why not start now? If that scares you to death, try this: Don't attempt to be something you're not. Women want you to be comfortable with yourself.

No, I'm serious; we really do.

Here is some advice based on things my girlfriends and I have noticed about guys who try too hard on dates. I hope it will give you some insight into the female mind and how we view you.

- **Be careful with how you compliment us.** Women do love a nice compliment or even two, but make them observational and casual. For example, when you pick your date up, you could say, "Wow, I like your dress. You look really pretty tonight!" Not, "Oh, that perfume you're wearing reminds me of my mother. She's in the car and she can't wait to meet you." Okay, speaking of mothers, *we don't want to be yours.*

Another point about moms is this: Do not tell us that we're just like your dear old mom! That's scary. On the other hand, don't talk about how no one could ever measure up to your mom or her cooking and housekeeping skills. We'll assume you're hiring a maid, not looking for a girlfriend. Some men can be really attached to their moms and not realize it. If you mention to us that you call your mom every couple of days, we can live with that. If you and your mom take advantage of your mobile-to-mobile and free texting so you can be in touch every hour on the hour, that's scary.

Another thing is that a lot of you guys out there are putting the same expectations on us as you would on your mom, and that's not cool. You want us to measure up to the fantasy you have of the woman who gave you life. That's also scary. It's nice to see your softer side and how you care for your mom, but if you go too far, we'll be reminded of a nice young son named Norman Bates, who ran a motel with his mom. Check out Mr. Alfred Hitchcock's telling version of this little tale. Save your "mother" issues for the professionals.

- **Don't try to be overly spiritual.** Guys have said some of the scariest things thinking they were being godly, like, "God told me you and I were supposed to be together." One guy actually used *The Passion of the Christ* to get me to go out with him. He had been calling and bugging me and he wasn't getting the hint that I wasn't interested, so one day he cornered me at a café and said, "Kerri, I challenge you to come to see *The Passion of the Christ* with me if you're Christian enough. I think you're the kind of woman who can take it. I really like you a lot!" Wow. Bold move, but one that was completely out of line, if you ask me.

- **Try to be in a good mood and see things in a positive light on your dates.** My friends and I have stories of going out with guys who acted like they hated the whole world and didn't even want to be out with us. They barked orders at waitresses and complained about every little thing. They said things like, "Man, I hate this place. I don't know why we came here. The food sucks and the service is terrible." We're thinking, *Well, you picked it out, crazy!* If we think you have anger issues with the waitress, how do you think we'll assume you're going to treat us? This is not good. Then, after this type of behavior, these guys try to lay it on really thick about how much they like us and how great they think the date is going. We don't buy it. If you're rude to others in our presence, we picture a Lifetime movie before our eyes, and you are the bad guy.

I could go on, but I think these few examples make my point perfectly clear. If you see yourself in any of these scenarios, then just be glad you're reading this book.

Okay, so here are some things you should never do. If you really like a girl and want the date to go great, that's fine. Go ahead and tell her. But don't put pressure on her to say the same thing right back.

Don't say things like, "You know, Kaitlyn, until I met you I didn't believe in fairy tales. I thought love was for the birds. But now I know why fools fall in love." Please don't quote bad song lyrics EVER. I repeat EVER. That is not why Bryan Adams wrote his songs. [Or Richard Marx, for you old people who know that "Hold On to the Nights" was a classic love ballad never to be touched or sung by any person other than dear old Richard].

And never quote Scripture. Seriously, I'm not saying this to shun the Bible. It's cool to talk to us about your faith and favorite Scriptures. We want to know about your relationship with God. Just don't use it to manipulate us into going out with you or to come across as übergodly. We'll see right through it. Don't say, "Do you like the water they served us? It reminds me of the time Peter walked on water. Would you walk on water if I asked you to?" That's scary. Some of you are reading this and thinking to yourself, *Are you kidding? Would any guy ever do that?* But just so you know, you are reading actual quotes.

Speaking of bad dates, you men have to learn to use your observation skills to determine if you're being scary. When you're on a date, try to gauge realistically how it's going. If you think she's bored and she doesn't make any suggestions for seeing you again even after you bring it up, just realize that she's not that into you. Don't call her seventeen times to ask her out again. If a girl wants to go out with you again, she will call you back. She will return your e-mails and faxes and text messages. Do not EVER look up a girl's phone number and call her if she didn't personally give it to you. Don't check out MapQuest to see how far apart your houses are or ask her landlord if there are any apartments open in her building after only a week of dating. These things all make you seem scary.

This brings me to my next point: Just because something looks good in the movies doesn't mean you should try it. You're not Patrick Swayze, and this is not the Catskills. Busting into your date's sister's wedding, saying, "I always do the last dance around here," and pulling your date away from the corner buffet table isn't a good idea. I know you see us girls swooning over TV and movies, but you can't expect to behave like the guys you see on sitcoms who lie, cheat, and stalk women all in a matter of twenty-two minutes and then wrap it up with uproarious laughter because they end up dressing in drag and getting caught by the downstairs landlord, Mr. Furley, who secretly thinks they look good in tights.

Hollywood gives you men false messages like if you're cute and funny or have six-pack abs, you can behave like a total stalker idiot and we won't care. [Okay, okay, some women wouldn't care if they found Ben Affleck in their bushes.] The reality is that we don't want to date guys like this because they're just as crazy as can be. It's all about common sense and a little bit of timing.

Guys, try not to rush God's timing. I know we women are known for rushing things, especially relationships. I'm aware that it's easy for you guys to want to cut to the chase too. But please take the suggestions I've given so you can get to the place where girls aren't scared to spend time with you and can truly get to know the real you. They'll realize you are sweet and caring and eager to please.

Be Lazy

[by Kerri]

I want to share the most dreaded words in the vocabulary of dating that you can say to a woman. I know what you're thinking, and they're not, "You look fat! I'm leaving you!" Rather, these particular words are usually spoken when you show up at her door for your date. They are, "I don't know; what do *you* want to do?"

This will sink the heart of any woman you're trying to impress, and she will consider you lazy because it shows that you have taken absolutely no time to plan this date. Guys, all we women want is to know you care. We want to know you've taken a few minutes to think things through when you ask us out on a date. It's not like we expect fancy gifts and roses every time, but when you leave all the planning and preparations to us, it gets really old. So many of my girlfriends have said this very same thing. They just want a guy to ask them out and then make a plan. We don't care if it's a movie that you chose at the dollar theater; at least you made an effort.

I know a lot of times we women can seem really picky. You'll say to us, "Hey, why don't we go out for Chinese?" and we'll say, "No, I hate Chinese; you know that!" I'm not saying we're perfect and that every idea you come up with will be met with smiles. But give us some benefit of the doubt that we won't shoot down all your suggestions. Some of us will be grateful that you're stepping up to the plate.

Early on in the dating process, it's really a very attractive quality, old-fashioned as it may seem, for the man to choose what activity the couple will do on their dates. So let's say you're on one of your first few dates with a girl. If you call her and ask her out for Friday, you can say on the phone, "Hey, would you like to go to a movie with me on Friday? I heard that new film by Spielberg looks pretty good." Then, if you're comfortable, you might say, "I'd like to take you to dinner beforehand. I know this little Italian place in your neighborhood. Do you like Italian?" Boys, this is music to our ears. This may seem like an old-fashioned request, but trust me, guys, 99 percent of women want to be pursued, and this is a perfect example of one way to do it. It's not exactly about what you plan; but it's that you have a plan at all. It shows us you're not lazy. Don't be that guy who calls a woman and says, "Hey! My roommate is out of town tonight. Want to hang out at my place or whatever? Why don't you drive over?"

In case you guys are stretched for creative ideas, here are some old standbys that my girlfriends have agreed are pretty much a sure thing to win a woman's affections:

- **Cards and notes.** Women love these. She wants to hear how fabulous you think she is. If you write it down, she can then show all her friends and also have something to stare at when she's not with you. This also comes in handy if you make her mad, because she may glance at your sweet card and forgive you more quickly.

- **Flowers she likes.** Regular red roses can always work, of course, but she wants you to notice which flowers she especially likes, such as daisies or sunflowers, and show some effort in getting them. And note that picking them from someone else's yard is not considered romantic; it's cheap.

- **Scavenger hunt.** This is a fun way to celebrate a birthday or special occasion. Leave notes around her house leading her to a special gift at the end. Or you can leave clues that lead to different locations in her neighborhood, ending up at a place that is special for the two of you or perhaps a manicure or something she enjoys that you have already arranged for her.

- **Involving her friends.** Let's say your special lady is turning thirty or something big like that. Ask her friends to help you plan a dinner or some sort of surprise for her. It can be as simple as having all her friends meet you at a particular pizza place she loves and bringing a cake. She'll love the effort you put into it and also the fact that all her friends know how much you adore her.

- **Picnics.** This is a no-fail activity. Girls love this. We see it in movies, and it's affordable. Round up a basket and some sandwiches, and you're good to go. If you live near a beach, get a pail and shovel and make sand castles. It's creative and fun. It might seem cliché, but trust me, it's a winner.

- **Fun activities, like going to an arcade, mini golfing, or go-cart racing.** These are fun, non-threatening ways to spend time together and see how competitive your lovely lady really is. Ron and I used to make fun wagers on our mini-golf games, like the loser had to buy lunch. Activities like these are great ways to be a kid again, and they're more creative than just watching a movie.
- **Comedy clubs or live theater.** Check your local paper to see what places have free tickets or discounts and take her for a night out. She'll love getting dressed up and seeing that you have some class.
- **Museums.** You'll appear really cultured. If you want to cheat, google the artist beforehand and then throw out a few facts on his or her work. Very cool.
- **Going out to eat at a place no one knows about.** Do some research or ask around. Find the best mom-and-pop pizza place and make it your special place to go. Plan an adventure to find the city's greatest brownie sundae or pizza pie or whatever the two of you enjoy.
- **Taking a class together.** Community centers offer classes on everything from cooking to salsa dancing. This will really show your sensitive side, especially if you're willing to rip it up on the dance floor with her and the instructors.

SOME BASIC "DON'T" ADVICE FOR GUYS

[because I (Matthew) think
healthy and successful dating begins with a few basics]

Don't date a girl *just to date a girl*. No matter how sexy or fun she may be, don't stay with her thinking that it will turn into something more. In the end, you will only hurt her. And that kind of guy is really just a jerk.

Don't sacrifice friendships just to be with her. Now, you have to use some judgment with this one because it's a bit touchy! But here it goes: You might think she's your world, but that doesn't mean she should replace everyone in it. It took me a long time to realize that it was okay to hang with the guys once in a while. And, heck, she'll probably realize she needs time away from you, too.

Don't keep calling! Come on, bro; if she doesn't answer, I'm sure she has a good reason. Trust me, I know how the mind can create off-the-wall scenarios, but you're more than likely over-reacting. Stop worrying. She isn't kissing her college art professor. She isn't in the middle of a bank robbery. And believe me when I say that she isn't fantasizing about your best friend. Oh, wait. I guess that could happen.

Don't rush "I love you." Some guys say it to score. Others say it because they believe they mean it. And still others say it because they really don't have anything else to say. Yet after those three little words are said, a world of changes often occurs. If you say it on the spur of the moment, you are in for trouble. Make sure you mean it! Make sure you really love her! If not, be prepared for another bad breakup.

Don't be the jealous type. If you find yourself buffing up any time a man talks to your girl, stop and take in a few deep breaths. Have a little more confidence, man. She's with you, not him. If you let her see that you're jealous, she will see only the insecure side of you. And I hate to break this to you but jealousy is one of the behaviors professionals look for when domestic violence is suspected. So, again, don't be a jerk!

Don't say, "I think she's the one," after the first date. I tell you this only to save you from the laughter you will hear when you let this stupid line fall out of your mouth. It will do more than just hit the floor. It will shatter into a million jokes, and your friends will probably bring up a lot of past relationship stories. I made the mistake of saying this after the first date with a girl. And you know what? By the second date I was sick of her. Believe me, a lot of us have made this mistake in the past. You don't necessarily have to!

RESIST GODLINESS IN A RELATIONSHIP

True godliness leaves the world convinced beyond
a shadow of a doubt that the only explanation for you
is Jesus Christ to whose eternally unchanging and
altogether adequate "I AM!" your heart has learned
to say with unshatterable faith, "Thou art!"

W. IAN THOMAS, *THE MYSTERY OF GODLINESS*

Almost every woman I interviewed for this book desires a man who pursues godly behavior. What do you believe godliness is? Is it simply how you live your life? Is it what you believe? Is it something that happens when you make a decision to join the journey with Jesus? Is godliness a synonym of holiness? Is it all of these answers?

Okay, now think about this question: In light of how you define what it means to be godly, how can you apply godliness to your pursuit of a healthy and successful relationship? Write your answer here:

It's probably not that difficult for you to apply your definition to at least some parts of your relationships. I mean, most Christians believe that to be godly within the confines of an unmarried relationship most definitely means to not engage in sexual behavior. But Christians define sex a bit differently. Some draw the line at kissing; for others, the line is drawn at oral sex.* [A broad spectrum, huh? Most of you probably agree that an opportunity for godly behavior exists somewhere in the mix.] Of course, most Christians would also agree that godliness includes

---

* For more information about sexuality, please check out Matthew's book *What You Didn't Learn from Your Parents About Sex* (Colorado Springs, CO: NavPress/TH1NK, 2006).

how we treat people, so naturally, how a guy treats his girlfriend would be included, don't you think? Consider these simple ideas of how treating your girlfriend in a godly way might be lived out every day:

- Put her first [a selfless heart].
- Serve her [a giving heart].
- Unconditionally love her [a forgiving heart].
- Compliment her [an encouraging heart].
- Touch her nonsexually [a pure heart].

For most of us, it's rather simple to think of how godliness fits into an actual dating relationship. But since you're reading this book, there's a pretty good chance that you're not dating, that you're reading this book in hopes that it will help you figure out *why* you're not dating.

Guys, the truth is, I don't know why you're not dating. I could take a few guesses, but that would be pretty pointless. But hopefully within the pages of this book you've been able to identify a few glaring personal characteristics that might be causing you issues in your dating life. If I have learned anything over the years about embracing godliness in all the different areas of my life, it's this: It's about the condition of my heart.

When Jesus spoke to people, many of his talks centered on the condition of a person's heart. Godliness begins with the heart in any situation, including our pursuit of healthy and successful dating. Jesus teaches us in Mark 7:21-22 that "from within, out of a person's heart, come evil thoughts, sexual immorality, theft, murder, adultery, greed, wickedness, deceit, lustful desires, envy, slander, pride, and foolishness." If you desire to pursue godliness in your relationships, godliness must begin in you.

 QUESTIONS TO CONSIDER:

- How can a Christian guy pursue godliness in relationships?
- Is it truly possible to earn godliness? If so, how?
- If you're in a relationship with a woman who doesn't encourage godliness, what should you do?

THESE ARE NOT GODLY!

[and between you and me, they're very unattractive]

- **Pride.** Yes, we know you *think* you're godly, but please don't think *too* highly of yourself.

- **Knowing it all.** You may, but you don't have to act like it.

- **Judgment.** Yeah, you're no doubt capable, but you're not qualified.

Now, even if you follow every bit of this advice, you might not instantly get a dating life. But try to learn to be content. I know that's easy for me to say because I'm married, but I didn't get married until I was almost thirty-one, so I know what might be happening in your life. I know that eventually you'll long for the companionship of a woman. And you might even be thinking, *Gosh, I think I'm ready to settle down.* And believe it or not, that's not a bad thing, though sometimes our culture makes it out to be. To be honest, that feeling is natural and normal and good!

However, when we guys are single, ready to get married, and itching for a little physical attention inside the confines of a committed relationship, we sometimes have a tendency to do stupid things. We get needy or emotionally dependent or angry or just plain weird. Believe me, at some point in my single life [and even now in my married life], I experienced all those feelings. I wish I knew a magic formula that could make them stop, but unfortunately I don't.

When I was in that situation, I would pray, and praying sometimes seemed to bring me out of my slump. But you know, sometimes I would pray, and afterward I still felt as frustrated as before. Do I understand why that is? No. Do I think it was a lack of faith? No. Do I think I was praying for the wrong thing? Maybe. But I don't believe God held that against me.

All I can say is that you should keep engaging the story of Jesus. Keep learning more about yourself. Keep thinking and rethinking ways that you might be able to better your ability to pursue relationships. And, perhaps most important, go out and enjoy life. Go on vacations. Go do things that old married folk can't do because they are tied down to a spouse or a family.

Sure, there's a part of you that wants to be tied down too. But for now, that's not for you. Don't waste your time. I needed to become content with being single, which honestly took a long time. But once I took a few steps toward contentment, I began to live a fuller life. I had a good time. I served as many people as I could. I worked my butt off. I went on a cruise — and, no, not a singles' cruise.

And after a while, I met an amazing girl named Jessica, whose joy and story came into my life and changed it forever.

Will it work out like that for you? Maybe not. But you never know; it might. All I do know is that either way, I am so glad I didn't just sit around and do nothing and wait for God to drop a person into my life. I really don't think God's going to drop a person into your life either, so I hope you'll take the advice in this book and the wisdom of the Spirit and go find yourself a hot wife.

Oh, and one more thing: Dude, lose the unibrow, whiten the teeth, and wax that back of yours. Trust me, it can't hurt! Well, waxing does hurt, but the pain is worth it.

CONGRATULATIONS! YOU HAVE SUCCESSFULLY COMPLETED TRAINING ON HOW TO RUIN YOUR DATING LIFE!

IN CONCLUSION

Can you believe you've made it this far? Congratulations for not throwing this book away after the first section. Now all your problems are solved. As long as you don't do any of the things we've mentioned in the previous sections and conduct yourself as that perfect God-fearing Christian we know you are deep down inside, you should be married and living happily ever after in less than thirty days. [But don't sue us if that doesn't happen.]

The truth is, we have no idea when you'll get married or what God has planned for your dating life. But we hope that by shedding some light on the common mistakes most Christians make in dating, we've set you up for a new beginning. Doesn't it feel strangely liberating to know your issues a little bit better? Do you quickly become codependent? Are you lazy? Do you use sexuality to get your way? Those are definitely hard questions, but answering them with the help of some good old self-reflection is, as you know, essential to correcting some past mistakes and preventing future ones. No, self-awareness is not a foolproof way to finding your mate, and just because you know about your commonly made mistakes doesn't mean you won't indulge in a moment or two of weakness. That, friends, is what makes us so hopelessly human. But since you've completed this entire book, we believe you are serious about setting yourself on the path to a healthy dating relationship.

There's one last piece of advice I (Kerri) would like to leave you with on how to ruin your dating life: *Don't wait on God. Go about things your own way.* As you can easily tell by my many embarrassing [and unfortunately very true] stories, I have chronically chosen my own way. And every time I followed my own instincts in dating, my next disaster was inevitably right around the corner. Whether it was through missionary dating with Jews for Kerri or my savior complex, I went on for years making my own choices and decisions, finally going to God in the last minute for help when I'd dug myself into another hole. The funny thing was that he always came through. He never turned his back and said, "Well, you've done it this time, Kerri. I'm sick of bailing you out time after time. Don't come crying to me now. You can just stay with Mr. Right Now for another two years for all I care."

Of course he never said any such thing. He knew that the tears behind my feeble dating attempts were real and that my heart wanted to get it right eventually. He knew I had good intentions, and every time I fell he was there to pick me up again like the loving Father he is. He honored my prayers and taught me to lean on him in this area of my life that was *so* tough to submit. What he really wanted me to do was lay my whole pursuit of dating and human love at his awesome altar so he could walk me through his plan, instead of the other way around.

Some people think God doesn't really care about or get involved in our dating endeavors. That's debatable, I suppose, except that God says he cares even about the sparrow's little life. And I know he wants you to experience the kind of relationship he uses as a metaphor for his own relationship with believers. I can't help but believe that God really does care about your dating life and all it entails. He knows the pain of being alone and the difficulty of having hope at times. He knows you sometimes just need to eat the whole package of cookies or the entire carton of ice cream or pick up the PlayStation controller to soothe your soul. It's all good. He recognizes the torture of going on bad blind date after bad blind date. He's up in heaven feeling your pain. Okay, sometimes he's up there laughing. It depends on the date.

I know it's a bit corny and overused in the church, but some clichés are cliché because they're true: Proverbs 3:5-6 is for you and is relevant to your dating life:

Trust in the LORD with all your heart
    and lean not on your own understanding;
in all your ways acknowledge him,
    and he will make your paths straight. (NIV)

I always take that verse personally, and as they sometimes teach us to do in Sunday school, I insert my name: "Kerri, trust in me and lean not on your human way of logic. I'm bigger than all of the world's wisdom, and I will guide you every step of the way."

So that is the best advice I can ever hope to give, which is fitting, I suppose, since it's not my own material.

ABOUT THE AUTHORS

MATTHEW PAUL TURNER has written fourteen books, including *The Christian Culture Survival Guide, What You Didn't Learn from Your Parents About Sex*, and the forthcoming *Jesus Needs New PR*. He lives in Nashville, Tennessee, with his wife, Jessica. For more information about him or to contact him, visit MatthewPaulTurner.com or MySpace.com/MatthewPaulTurner.

KERRI POMAROLLI is an accomplished actress, published author, speaker, and veteran of television with too many credits to mention [says her publicist]. She has written and contributed to several books, and her articles regularly appear in magazines such as *Brio* and *Radiant*. She is a frequent guest on hundreds of radio and television programs and networks, including *The Tonight Show*, Hallmark, CNN, ABC Family, Lifetime, and CBN. Kerri is in high demand as a headliner and keynote speaker and tours throughout the U.S. and Canada, using humor and innovative evangelism to inspire others to embrace a God-filled life. She lives by the sea in California with her crazy comic husband, Ron McGehee, and sometimes they dance in the kitchen. She is also available for weddings and bar mitzvahs.

For more information on booking Kerri, contact Rhonda Boudreaux/CFA Productions at 1-877-773-4242. You can learn more about Kerri at www.kerripom.com.

CHECK OUT THESE OTHER GREAT TITLES FROM NAVPRESS!

The Singlehood Phenomenon
Dr. Beverly Rodgers and Dr. Tom Rodgers
ISBN-13: 978-1-57683-884-6
ISBN-10: 1-57683-884-6

Drs. Beverly and Tom Rodgers address the top ten reasons singles aren't getting married and show how societal trends make finding a soul mate that much more difficult. Learn how to integrate psychological principles and biblical truths to develop healthy, godly love relationships.

What You Didn't Learn from Your Parents About Sex
Matthew Paul Turner
ISBN-13: 978-1-57683-940-9
ISBN-10: 1-57683-940-0

With his signature style and humorous insights, Matthew Paul Turner tackles tough issues that can lead to a better understanding of God's plan for sex, despite the awkward sex talk.

5 Paths to the Love of Your Life
Winner, Chediak, Holland, Wilson, Clark, Lindvall
ISBN-13: 978-1-57683-709-2
ISBN-10: 1 57683-709-2

Dating, relationships, and marriage are all too important to risk on one person's unproven advice. In 5 Paths to the Love of Your Life, respected relationship experts and best-selling authors help you gain new insight into dating and marriage. They offer you sound advice grounded in biblical truth and gleaned from their own personal experiences.

To order copies, visit your local Christian bookstore,
call NavPress at 1-800-366-7788, or log on to www.navpress.com.

To locate a Christian bookstore near you, call 1-800-991-7747.